THE **TESTING** SERIES

ARMED FORCES **TESTS**

THE **TESTING** SERIES
expert advice on test preparation

how2become

134201 ✓

CV PS NL 355.0076 ARM
Armed Forces
Selection Test
British Army
Royal Navy
Royal Air Force
Selection Process

Orders: Please contact How2become Ltd,
Suite 2, 50 Churchill Square Business Centre, Kings Hill, Kent ME19 4YU.

Telephone: (44) 0845 643 1299 - Lines are open Monday to Friday 9am until 5pm.
Fax: (44) 01732 525965.
You can also order via the email address info@how2become.co.uk.

ISBN: 978-1907558092

First published 2010

Typeset for How2become Ltd by Good Golly Design, Canada, goodgolly.ca.

Printed in Great Britain for How2become Ltd
by Bell & Bain Ltd, 303 Burnfield Road, Thornliebank, Glasgow G46 7UQ.

CONTENTS

INTRODUCTION   **V**

PREFACE
BY AUTHOR RICHARD MCMUNN   **VI**

CHAPTER 1
ABOUT THE SELECTION TEST FOR THE ARMED FORCES   **1**

CHAPTER 2
THE BRITISH ARMY RECRUIT BATTERY TEST   **5**

CHAPTER 3
THE ROYAL NAVY RECRUITING TEST   **69**

CHAPTER 4
THE ROYAL AIR FORCE AIRMAN/AIRWOMAN TEST   **139**

INTRODUCTION

Dear Sir/Madam,

Welcome to your new guide, Armed Forces Tests: Practice Tests for the Army, RAF and Royal Navy. This guide contains hundreds of sample test questions that are appropriate for anyone who is applying to join any of the three UK Armed Forces.

The selection tests for the Armed Forces are designed to assess potential employees 'suitability' for specific posts. In the majority of cases, the higher scores you achieve, the more job opportunities you will have at your disposal. This is particularly true of the British Army Recruit Battery Test (BARB). Whilst the minimum pass mark for entry in the Army is 26, a candidate will need to score far higher if he or she wishes to join a regiment such as the Royal Electrical and Mechanical Engineers. The key to success is to try your hardest to get 100% correct answers in the test that you are undertaking. If you aim for 100% in your preparation, then you are far more likely to achieve the trade or career that you want. We have deliberately supplied you with lots of sample questions to assist you. It is crucial that when you get a question wrong, you take the time to find out why you got it wrong. Understanding the question is very important.

Finally, even if you are applying for the RAF, you should still try the questions in the guide that are designed for the Royal Navy and the Army, and vice versa. You will find that the more practice you undertake in the build up to the real test, the better you will perform on the day.

Good luck and best wishes,

The how2become team

The how2become team

PREFACE
BY RICHARD MCMUNN

It's probably important that I start off by explaining a little bit about myself, my background, and also why I'm suitably qualified to help you pass the selection tests that form part of the Armed Forces.

At the time of writing I am 38 years old and live in the sea-side town of Whitstable which is located on the North Kent coast. I left school at the usual age of 16 and joined the Royal Navy, serving on-board HMS Invincible as part of 800 Naval Air Squadron which formed part of the Fleet Air Arm. There I was at the age of 16, travelling the world and working as an engineer on Sea Harrier jets! It was fantastic and I loved every minute of it. After four years I left the Royal Navy and joined Kent Fire and Rescue Service as a firefighter. Over the next 17 years I worked my way up through the ranks to the position of Assistant Divisional Officer. During my time in the Fire Service I spent a lot of time working as an instructor at the Fire Brigade Training Centre. I was also involved in the selection process for assessing candidates who wanted to join the job as a firefighter. Therefore, my knowledge and experience gained so far in life has been invaluable in helping people like you to pass any type of selection process. I am sure you will find this guide an invaluable resource during your preparation for joining the Armed Forces.

I have always been fortunate in the fact that I persevere at everything I do. I understand that if I keep working hard in life then I will always be successful; or I will achieve whatever it is that I want to achieve. This is an important lesson that I want you to take on-board straight away. If you work hard and

 THE **TESTING** SERIES

persevere, then success will come your way. The same rule applies whilst applying for a career in the Armed Forces; if you work hard and try lots of test questions, then you will be successful.

Finally, it is very important that you believe in your own abilities. It does not matter if you have no qualifications. It does not matter if are currently weak in the area of psychometric testing. What does matter is self-belief, self-discipline and a genuine desire to improve and become successful.

Best wishes,

Richard McMunn

CHAPTER 1
ABOUT THE SELECTION TESTS FOR THE ARMED FORCES

Psychometric tests have been in use in the Armed Forces for many years. They are simply used as a tool to assess a candidates 'ability' to perform specific tasks that are similar to the ones they will have to undertake in a real life scenario. If we break down the word 'psychometric' we can see that 'psycho' means mind and 'metric' means to measure.

The selection tests vary depending on whether you are applying to join the Army, the Royal Air Force or the Royal Navy. Unsurprisingly, the tests for the Royal Air Force are the toughest, simply because many of the roles within the Force are of a highly technical nature.

ARMY - THE BRITISH ARMY RECRUIT BATTERY TEST (BARB)

The BARB test is a computer-based, psychometric assessment that was developed by the Defence Evaluation and Research Agency (DERA) and Plymouth University. It is a series of timed questions that assess a candidate's ability to absorb information quickly and logically. The computer automatically calculates the candidate's score, based on the number of correct answers and the time taken. The final score is referred to as the GTI (General Trainability Index). The BARB test has been in use since July 1992.

The pass mark for the BARB test is currently 26 although you will need to confirm this with your local Armed Forces Careers Office. This effectively means that you must get 26 questions correct, but as I mentioned earlier don't just settle for a minimum pass. You need to achieve as high a score as possible as this will give you more career options depending on your academic results.

RAF – THE AIRMAN/AIRWOMAN SELECTION TEST

The Airman/Airwoman Selection Test (AST) consists of a number of different aptitude tests which are designed to assess which careers in the RAF you are most suited to. There are many different career opportunities available and each one requires a different level of skill. The AST consists of seven timed multiple choice aptitude tests as follows:

> A verbal reasoning test which assesses how well you can interpret written information. During this test you will have 15 minutes to answer 20 questions

> A numerical reasoning test which determines how accurately you can interpret numerical information such as charts, graphs and tables. The test will also assess your ability to use fractions, decimals and different formula. There are two parts to this test. During the first test you will have just 4 minutes to answer 12 questions that are based on fractions, decimals and formula. During the second test you will have 11 minutes to answer 15 questions that relate to different graphs and tables

> A work rate test which is used to assess how quickly and accurately you can carry out routine tasks. During this test you will have 4 minutes to answer 20 questions

> A spatial reasoning test designed to examine your ability to work with different shapes and objects. During this test you will have just 4 minutes to answer 10 questions

> A mechanical comprehension test which is used to assess how effectively you can work with different mechanical concepts. During this particular test you will have 10 minutes in which to answer 20 questions

> An electrical comprehension test which will assess your ability to work with different electrical concepts. During this test you will have 11 minutes to complete 21 questions

> A memory test which determines how accurately you can remember and recall information. There are two parts to this test and you will have a total of 10 minutes in which to answer 20 questions

ROYAL NAVY – THE ROYAL NAVY RECRUITING TEST

The main purpose of the Royal Navy Recruiting Test is to establish how effective you are at figuring out problems, how good you are at English and Mathematics, and if you can understand basic mechanical concepts. Just like the BARB tests, they show the Royal Navy what type of jobs you will most suited to. The Royal Navy Recruiting Test covers the following four areas

• A reasoning test (30 questions to be completed in 9 minutes)

• A verbal ability test (30 questions to be completed in 9 minutes)

• A numeracy test (30 questions to be completed in 16 minutes)

• A mechanical reasoning test (30 questions to be completed in 10 minutes)

The tests are usually carried out at the Armed Forces Careers Office and will be under strict timed conditions. Details of the time restrictions and number of questions per exercise will be provided in your recruitment literature. The pass mark for the RN Recruiting Test will very much depend on the technical ability level required for the post you are applying for; although a pass mark of 50% is normally sufficient for the majority of branches.

Now that we have taken the time to understand the different types of test that you will be required to sit during the selection process, let's now take a look at some sample test questions. I have dedicated different chapters to each testing area for all three of the Armed Forces.

Regardless of which service you are applying to join, I believe it is good practice to work through the sample tests for all three of the Armed Forces.

CHAPTER 2
THE BRITISH ARMY RECRUIT BATTERY TEST

One of the initial stages of the selection process will see a requirement for you to sit the British Army Recruit Battery Test. The test is more commonly known as the 'BARB test' and it has been in use for many years. It is a tried and tested method that the Army will use to determine what career(s) you are most likely to be suited to. It is important that you aim for the highest score possible on the test and this can only be achieved through 'deliberate' and 'repetitive' practice. Work hard at the tests within this guide and also within the BARB testing booklet that you will receive from the AFCO. Your choice of trade will be dependant upon the score you achieve during the BARB test. Basically, the higher your score, the more career options you will have. This is a good incentive for you to work hard and prepare fully.

Within this section of the guide I have provided you with a number of sample test questions to help you prepare for the real test. Please note that these are not the exact questions that you will be required to sit on the day. However, they are provided as a useful practice tool in order to help focus your mind on the type of tests you will be sitting. It is also important to point out that during the real test you may be required to answer the questions on a computer screen and how they will be presented will be different to how they are formatted within this guide. Take a look at the explanations provided and make sure you fully understand what is involved before attempting the questions. Once you have completed the sample questions it is important that you take note of where you have gone wrong. Learn from any mistakes you make as this will help you to further improve your scores during the real test.

Reasoning tests form an integral part of the BARB selection tests within the British Army selection process. These tests are relatively simple to understand once you fully appreciate what is required. The reasoning tests are basically a form of problem solving and you will be asked a number of questions, usually about a relationship between two people. For example, you could be asked a question along the following lines:

SAMPLE QUESTION

Stuart is taller than Mark. Who is shorter?

The answer in this case would be Mark as the statement suggests that Stuart is taller than Mark. Therefore Mark is the shorter of the two.

Answer: Mark

Here is another example:

Michelle is not as wealthy as Owen. Who has less money?

Answer: Michelle

The statement suggests that Michelle is not as wealthy as Owen, therefore Owen has more money.

When answering these questions it is important to READ each question thoroughly. The questions are relatively simple to answer but they can catch you out if you do not understand exactly what the question is asking.

COMPUTER BASED VERSION OF THE TEST

When you attend the careers office to sit the BARB test you may be asked to take the test on a computer. The computer version of the test will require you to use 'touch screen' answers, which means that instead of using a pen and paper to mark down your answers you will have to touch the computer screen instead. Whilst this is far quicker than writing down your answers, you will need to understand the questions fully before giving your answer.

The question on the screen may appear as follows:

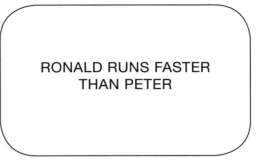

RONALD RUNS FASTER
THAN PETER

Once you have read the statement you will then need to touch the screen to obtain the question. Make certain that you remember the statement as once you touch the screen it will disappear and you will be provided with the question as follows:

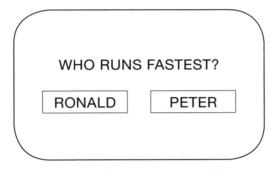

WHO RUNS FASTEST?

RONALD   PETER

Once the question appears you will then be required to touch the screen in order to indicate your answer. Can you remember what the question was? My tip is to repeat the statement at least three times in your head before touching the screen to obtain the question. Once the question appears you can repeat the statement to yourself that *Ronald runs faster than Peter* and therefore provide yourself with the answer to the question – **Ronald is the fastest.**

Once you fully understand what is required, move on to exercise 1 where you have 5 minutes in which to answer the 15 questions. Please note that the time limit placed on this exercise will not be the same as the one set during the real BARB test. Once you have completed the exercise make sure you check thoroughly any questions you got wrong. It is important to do this so that you can improve your scores during the real test.

ARMED FORCES **TESTS**

BARB TEST PRACTICE QUESTIONS REASONING TEST
EXERCISE 1

QUESTION 1

Sophie is not as tall as Andrew. Who is shorter?

Answer

QUESTION 2

Peter is wealthier than Roman. Who is the poorest?

Answer

QUESTION 3

Grace runs faster than Julie. Who runs the slowest?

Answer

QUESTION 4

Thomas is heavier than Fred. Who weighs the most?

Answer

QUESTION 5

Charlotte's house was less expensive than Margaret's. Whose house cost less?

Answer

QUESTION 6

Michael runs slower than his sister Paris. Who runs the fastest?

Answer

QUESTION 7

Lily has more money than Hugh. Who is poorer?

Answer

QUESTION 8

Amelia is stronger than Brian. Who is the strongest?

Answer

QUESTION 9

The red car is older than the green car. Which car is the youngest?

Answer

QUESTION 10

Ella's shoe size is 5 and Mary's is 8. Who needs the smaller size shoes?

Answer

QUESTION 11

Monty is sadder than William. Who is the happier of the two?

Answer

QUESTION 12

Rick works harder than Robert, but not as hard as Daniel. Who works the least?

Answer

QUESTION 13

Tim has 6 points on his licence and Pauline has 3 points on her licence. Who has the most points?

Answer

QUESTION 14

Mohammed eats faster than Lucy. Who eats the slowest?

Answer [   ]

QUESTION 15

Ailsa finishes reading the book after Tony. Who finished the book first?

Answer [   ]

Now that you have completed exercise 1, take the time to check over your answers carefully. If you got any wrong make sure you learn from your mistakes. This is a crucial part of your development.

ANSWERS TO REASONING TEST - EXERCISE 1

Question 1:   Sophie

Question 2:   Roman

Question 3:   Julie

Question 4:   Thomas

Question 5:   Charlotte's

Question 6:   Paris

Question 7:   Hugh

Question 8:   Amelia

Question 9:   Green car

Question 10: Ella

Question 11: William

Question 12: Robert

Question 13: Tim

Question 14: Lucy

Question 15: Tony

Once you are satisfied move on to the next exercise. Once again you have 5 minutes to answer the 15 questions.

BARB TEST PRACTICE QUESTIONS REASONING TEST
EXERCISE 2

QUESTION 1

The blue car is twice as fast as the black car. Which car is slowest?

Answer

QUESTION 2

Addison has more hair than Oscar. Who has the least hair?

Answer

QUESTION 3

Steven worked for 3 hours and ten minutes whilst Tony worked for 195 minutes? Who worked the longest?

Answer

QUESTION 4

Alice passed her driving test in 1971 and her husband Derek passed his in 1970. Who has held their driving licence the least amount of time?

Answer

QUESTION 5

Rebecca lives 26 miles away from her place of work. Sue's workplace is 24 miles away from her home. Who lives the least distance from their place of work?

Answer

QUESTION 6

Rupert has a yacht which cost him £12,750. Tyrone has a yacht which cost him £12,725. Who has the most expensive yacht?

Answer [   ]

QUESTION 7

Timothy weighs slightly less than Simon. Who is the lightest?

Answer [   ]

QUESTION 8

Marcus's house was built in June 1923 and his girlfriend Jennifer's house was built in July 1923. Who has the oldest house?

Answer [   ]

QUESTION 9

Rita spends £16.89 at the shops and Katie spends £16.98. Who spends the least amount?

Answer [   ]

QUESTION 10

Rodney started work at 9am and finished at 5.10pm. Gary started work at 8.50am and finished at 16.55pm. Who worked for the least amount of time?

Answer [   ]

QUESTION 11

Roy joined the Army on May the 8th 1994 and left 12 years later. Mary joined the Army on May the 18th 1995 and left on May the 20th 2007. Who stayed in the Army for the least amount of time?

Answer

QUESTION 12

Alan has been in the Army for two years. Victor has been in the Army for 729 days. Who has been in the Army for the least amount of time?

Answer

QUESTION 13

Ruth is poorer than Charlene. Who is the wealthier?

Answer

QUESTION 14

Wendy rides her bike twice the speed of Uma. Who rides their bike the slowest?

Answer

QUESTION 15

Daisy takes out a loan for £4,500 over 60 months. Anthony takes out a loan for £5,000 over 48 months. Whose loan will take the least amount of time to pay back?

Answer

Once again, take the time to check over your answers carefully correcting any that you have got wrong before moving onto the next exercise.

ANSWERS TO REASONING TEST - EXERCISE 2

Question 1:   Black car

Question 2:   Oscar

Question 3:   Tony

Question 4:   Alice

Question 5:   Sue

Question 6:   Rupert

Question 7:   Timothy

Question 8:   Marcus

Question 9:   Rita

Question 10: Gary

Question 11: Roy

Question 12: Victor

Question 13: Charlene

Question 14: Uma

Question 15: Anthony

BARB TEST PRACTICE QUESTIONS
LETTER CHECKING TEST

When you come to sit the BARB test you will be asked to answer questions that require you to check letters. The aim of this test is to see how fast you can check information that is presented before you. Whilst working in the Army you will be often required to carry out specific tasks which involve the accurate checking of information, equipment and data.

The following is an example of a letter checking question:

SAMPLE QUESTION

R	t	W	f	u
r	p	M	F	U

How many letters match?

You can see from the above example that there are columns of letters. In the 1st, 4th and 5th columns are letters that are identical, albeit one letter is a capital and the other is not. The other two columns contain different letters and therefore do not match. It is your task to identify how many pairs of letters do match. In this case I have circled the correct answer for you as being 3 matching pairs.

During the real BARB test you will most probably be asked to sit the computer 'touch-screen' version of the test as opposed to writing down your answers.

When you carry out the test on the computer the question will be presented to you in a similar format to the following:

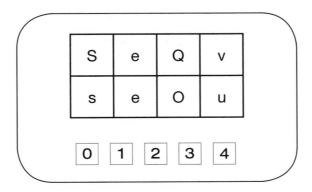

Underneath the letters you will notice a number of boxes giving you a choice of how many letters match. In this case the answer is 2 as the first two columns of letters match, whereas the last two do not. In this case you would touch the number '2' box on the screen as your answer. It is important that you work as quickly as possible because the more you score correct, the higher your result will be at the end. As always, deliberate and repetitive practice will serve well to increase your scores.

Tips for improving your score on the letter checking test

> When answering these questions you may find it useful to scan each line downwards in turn and keep a check of how many are correct. When you have scanned the final 4th line you will know how many are correct and then you can touch the number on the screen that corresponds to the correct answer.

> You will have very little time to answer as many as you can during the real test so you need to work quickly and as accurately as possible. Look out for letters that are similar but not the same, such as:

Q and O

G and Q

P and q

Now take a look at the first letter checking exercise on the following page and see how you get on. There are 15 questions and you have 5 minutes in which to answer them. Simply circle the correct answer with a pen or pencil.

BARB TEST PRACTICE QUESTIONS
LETTER CHECKING TEST - EXERCISE 1

QUESTION 1

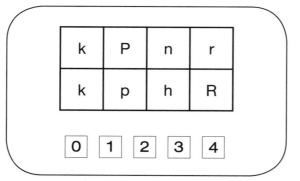

QUESTION 2

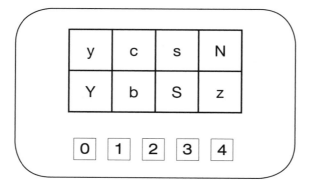

QUESTION 3

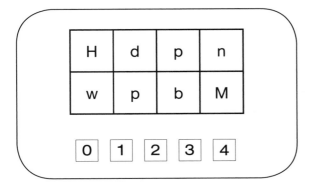

QUESTION 4

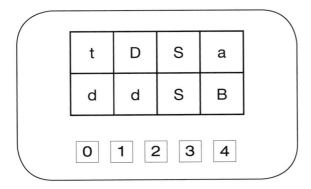

QUESTION 5

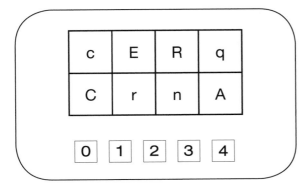

QUESTION 6

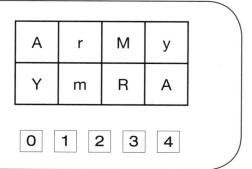

A	r	M	y
Y	m	R	A

0 1 2 3 4

QUESTION 7

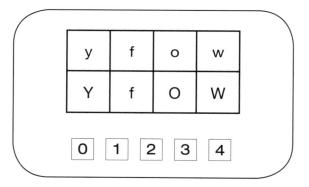

y	f	o	w
Y	f	O	W

0 1 2 3 4

QUESTION 8

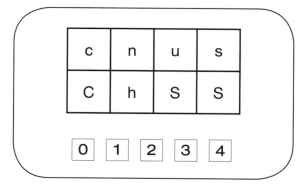

c	n	u	s
C	h	S	S

0 1 2 3 4

QUESTION 9

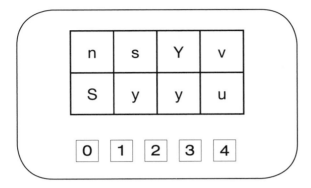

QUESTION 10

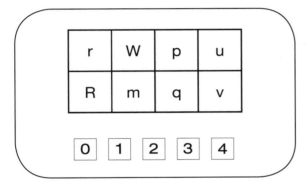

QUESTION 11

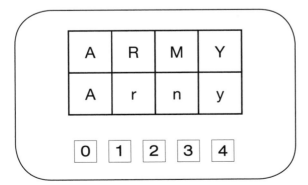

QUESTION 12

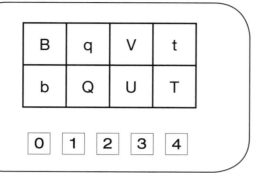

B	q	V	t
b	Q	U	T

0 1 2 3 4

QUESTION 13

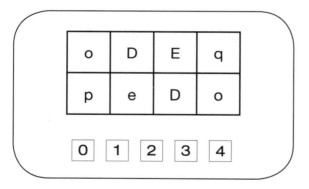

o	D	E	q
p	e	D	o

0 1 2 3 4

QUESTION 14

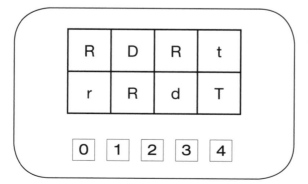

R	D	R	t
r	R	d	T

0 1 2 3 4

QUESTION 15

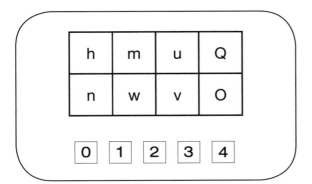

Now that you have completed the first letter checking exercise take the time to assess your performance with the answers provided. Once you are satisfied, move onto exercise number 2.

ANSWERS TO LETTER CHECKING TEST - EXERCISE 1

Question 1:   3

Question 2:   2

Question 3:   0

Question 4:   2

Question 5:   1

Question 6:   0

Question 7:   4

Question 8:   2

Question 9:   1

Question 10: 1

Question 11: 3

Question 12: 3

Question 13: 0

Question 14: 2

Question 15: 0

BARB TEST PRACTICE QUESTIONS
LETTER CHECKING TEST - EXERCISE 2

QUESTION 1

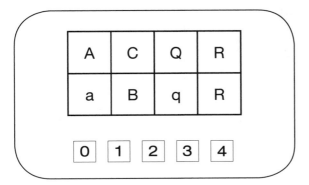

QUESTION 2

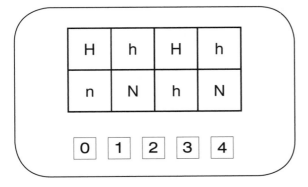

QUESTION 3

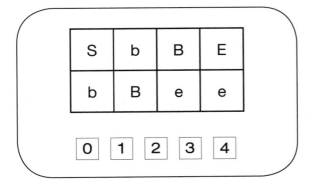

QUESTION 4

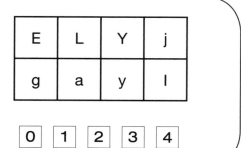

QUESTION 5

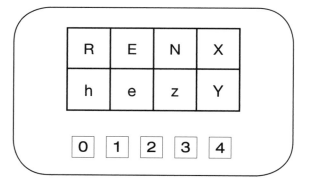

QUESTION 6

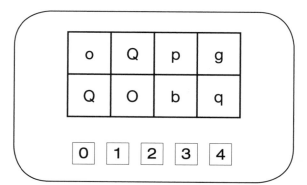

QUESTION 7

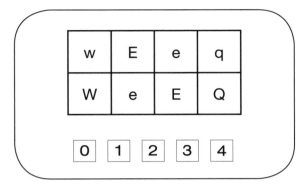

QUESTION 8

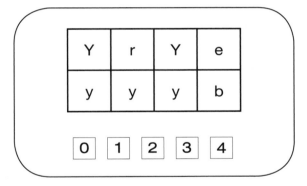

QUESTION 9

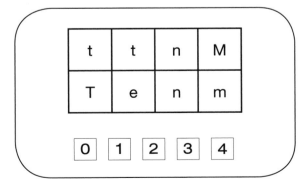

QUESTION 10

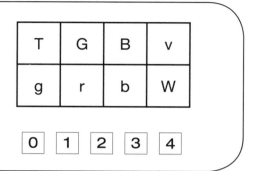

QUESTION 11

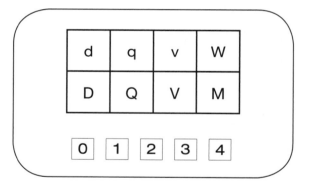

QUESTION 12

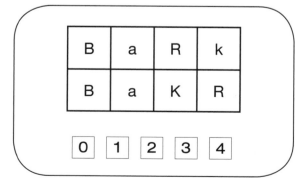

QUESTION 13

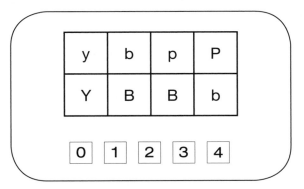

QUESTION 14

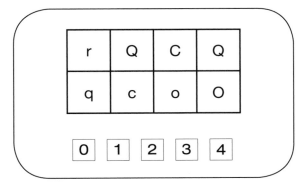

QUESTION 15

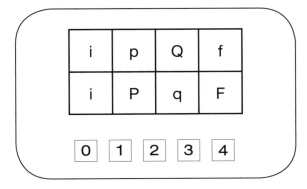

Once again, take the time to assess your performance with the answers provided. If you get any wrong make sure you return to the question and see where you need to improve.

ANSWERS TO LETTER CHECKING TEST - EXERCISE 2

Question 1:   3

Question 2:   1

Question 3:   2

Question 4:   1

Question 5:   1

Question 6:   0

Question 7:   4

Question 8:   2

Question 9:   3

Question 10: 1

Question 11: 3

Question 12: 2

Question 13: 2

Question 14: 0

Question 15: 4

BARB TEST PRACTICE QUESTIONS
DISTANCE NUMBER TEST

During the BARB Test you will have to sit what is called a Distance Number test. This test requires you to analyse three numbers and decide which one of the three fits a certain criteria. For example, you may find 3 numbers appear on your computer screen as follows:

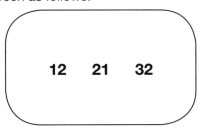

The numbers can appear in any order and will not necessarily increase in value as indicated above. You then have to analyse the numbers and decide which one is the largest number and which one is the smallest.

In this case that would be as follows:

Largest Value = 32
Smallest value = 12

This then leaves you with the number 21. Once you have decided which number remains (in this case the number 21) you must then decide which of the two numbers (12 and 32) is the furthest away from it, hence the title 'Distance Number' test. To work this out you can see that 12 is 9 away from 21 and 32 is 11 away from 21, therefore leaving you with the answer 32.

This may seem complicated at first but with a little practice you will soon grasp the concept of what is required. Try as many questions as possible and you will find that your scores will keep increasing. On the following pages I have provided you with a number of sample test questions to assist you. Before you start the test however take a look at the following four step approach that will help you to answer the questions.

Step 1
From the three numbers, decide which one is the smallest and which one is the largest

Step 2

Then look at the number you are left with

Step 3

Now decide which of the two numbers in step 1 is furthest away from the number in step 2

Step 4

The number that is the furthest away from the number in step 2 is the correct answer.

Now move on to exercise 1. There are 15 questions for you to try and you have 7 minutes in which to answer them. The times that are provided in this test are different to times allocated in the real BARB test. Calculators are not permitted.

BARB TEST PRACTICE QUESTIONS
DISTANCE NUMBER TEST - EXERCISE 1

QUESTION 1

4   8   10

Answer

QUESTION 2

2   9   3

Answer

QUESTION 3

1   5   2

Answer

QUESTION 4

21   2   42

Answer

QUESTION 5

16   5   35

Answer [   ]

QUESTION 6

43   70   98

Answer [   ]

QUESTION 7

101   4   98

Answer [   ]

QUESTION 8

12   50   89

Answer [   ]

QUESTION 9

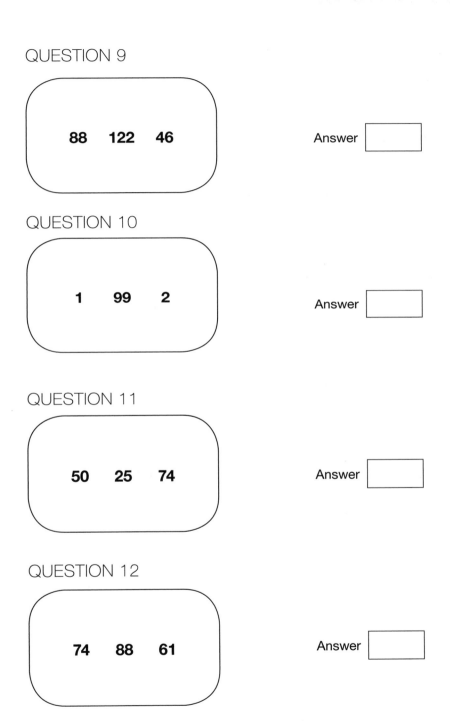

88   122   46

Answer [   ]

QUESTION 10

1   99   2

Answer [   ]

QUESTION 11

50   25   74

Answer [   ]

QUESTION 12

74   88   61

Answer [   ]

QUESTION 13

5   44   84

Answer

QUESTION 14

144   11   81

Answer

QUESTION 15

32   3   10

Answer

Now that you have completed the first distance number exercise work through your answers carefully to see which, if any, you got wrong.

ANSWERS TO DISTANCE NUMBER TEST - EXERCISE 1

Question 1:   4

Question 2:   9

Question 3:   5

Question 4:   42

Question 5:   35

Question 6:   98

Question 7:   4

Question 8:   89

Question 9:   46

Question 10: 99

Question 11: 25

Question 12: 88

Question 13: 84

Question 14: 11

Question 15: 32

Now move on to exercise 2. Again, there are 15 questions and you have 7 minutes in which to answer them. The times that are provided in this test are different to times allocated in the real test. Calculators are not permitted.

BARB TEST PRACTICE QUESTIONS
DISTANCE NUMBER TEST - EXERCISE 2

QUESTION 1

4   40   8

Answer ☐

QUESTION 2

12   16   19

Answer ☐

QUESTION 3

4   6   3

Answer ☐

QUESTION 4

111   114   112

Answer ☐

THE **TESTING** SERIES

QUESTION 5

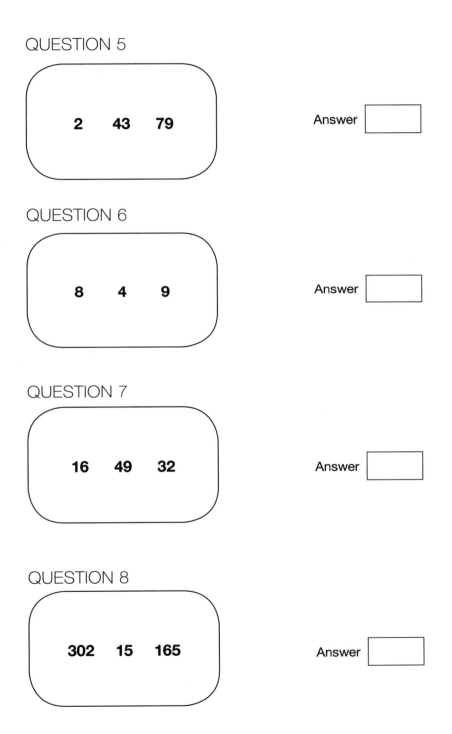

2   43   79

Answer

QUESTION 6

8   4   9

Answer

QUESTION 7

16   49   32

Answer

QUESTION 8

302   15   165

Answer

QUESTION 9

1   45   97

Answer

QUESTION 10

53   44   34

Answer

QUESTION 11

66   87   76

Answer

QUESTION 12

54   104   153

Answer

QUESTION 13

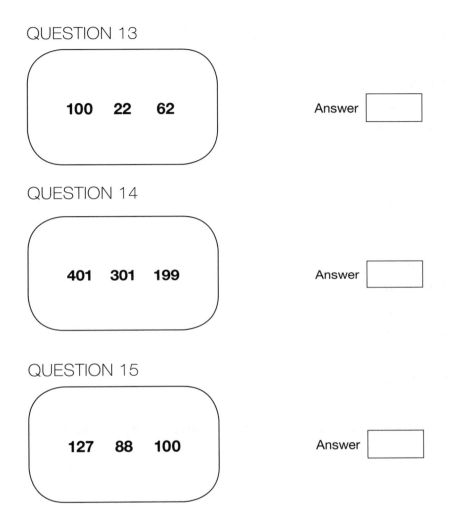

100   22   62

Answer

QUESTION 14

401   301   199

Answer

QUESTION 15

127   88   100

Answer

Now that you have completed exercise 2, work through your answers checking carefully to see which, if any, you got wrong.

ANSWERS TO DISTANCE NUMBER TEST - EXERCISE 2

Question 1:   40

Question 2:   12

Question 3:   6

Question 4:   114

Question 5:   2

Question 6:   4

Question 7:   49

Question 8:   15

Question 9:   97

Question 10: 34

Question 11: 87

Question 12: 54

Question 13: 22

Question 14: 199

Question 15: 127

Once you have checked your answers please move onto the next section of the guide.

BARB TEST PRACTICE QUESTIONS
SELECTING THE ODD ONE OUT

As part of the BARB test you will be required to sit a 'selecting the odd one out' test. The requirement of this test is to simply select the odd one out from a group of words. Take a look at the following sample question:

SAMPLE QUESTION

Which of the following is the odd one out?

Eyes   Ears   Carpet

The answer to this question is Carpet. The reason is that Ears and Eyes are associated together, whereas Carpet cannot be placed in the same category as the other two words, so therefore is the odd one out. You may find some words are the opposite of another one, which again is the association or connection. Here's another example.

SAMPLE QUESTION

Which of the following is the odd one out?

Cold   Hot   Spanner

The odd one out in this example is Spanner. Cold is opposite to Hot, so therefore Spanner is the odd one out. Now try the exercise that follows. Remember to read the questions carefully. When you sit the real test with the Army you may have to take the test on a computer. An example of a question presented on a computer screen would be as follows:

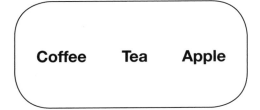

Coffee   Tea   Apple

In this particular question Apple is the odd one out, and therefore the box that you would touch on the screen during the computer version of the test.

Allow yourself 2 minutes to answer as many questions as possible on the following exercise which contains 14 questions. **Simply circle which word you believe is the odd one out.** The times provided in this sample test are different to the real test.

BARB TEST PRACTICE QUESTIONS
SELECTING THE ODD ONE OUT - EXERCISE 1

QUESTION 1

Apple   Cucumber   Banana

QUESTION 2

Grass   Soil   Shirt

QUESTION 3

Today   Tomorrow   Peaches

QUESTION 4

Red   Fun   Green

QUESTION 5

Car   Wheels   Swim

QUESTION 6

Track   Pillow   Train

QUESTION 7

Seeds   Allotment   Chimney

QUESTION 8

Pin   Loud   Quiet

QUESTION 9

Walk   Teach   Tutor

QUESTION 10

Gain   Loss   Wood

QUESTION 11

Intoxicated   Sober   Fly

QUESTION 12

Thoroughfare   Together   Apart

QUESTION 13

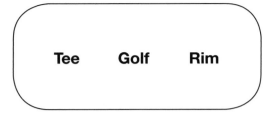

QUESTION 14

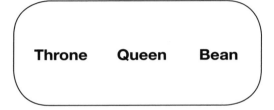

Now that you have completed the exercise, take your time to work through the answers carefully.

ANSWERS TO SELECTING THE ODD ONE OUT
EXERCISE 1

Question 1:   Cucumber

Question 2:   Shirt

Question 3:   Peaches

Question 4:   Fun

Question 5:   Swim

Question 6:   Pillow

Question 7:   Chimney

Question 8:   Pin

Question 9:   Walk

Question 10: Wood

Question 11: Fly

Question 12: Thoroughfare

Question 13: Rim

Question 14: Bean

Once you have checked all of your answers thoroughly move on to sample exercise 2. In this exercise there are 14 questions and you have 2 minutes in which to complete them.

BARB TEST PRACTICE QUESTIONS
SELECTING THE ODD ONE OUT - EXERCISE 2

QUESTION 1

Single   Married   Tax

QUESTION 2

Edge   Weak   Strong

QUESTION 3

Pencil   Right   Write

QUESTION 4

Ceiling   Wall   Litre

QUESTION 5

Kilo   Gram   Pick

QUESTION 6

Few   Drinks   Many

QUESTION 7

Siphon   Stern   Aft

QUESTION 8

Arm   Gun   Bullet

QUESTION 9

> **Terrible   Awful   Meaning**

QUESTION 10

> **Queue   Knowledge   Information**

QUESTION 11

> **Disdain   Disgrace   Youthful**

QUESTION 12

> **Snare   Rabbit   Piccolo**

QUESTION 13

Recorder   Optical   Trumpet

QUESTION 14

Till   Bake   Flour

Now that you have completed exercise 2, work through your answers carefully. Once you are satisfied move on to the next chapter of the guide.

ANSWERS TO SELECTING THE ODD ONE OUT
EXERCISE 2

Question 1:   Tax

Question 2:   Edge

Question 3:   Right

Question 4:   Litre

Question 5:   Pick

Question 6:   Drinks

Question 7:   Siphon

Question 8:   Arm

Question 9 :   Meaning

Question 10: Queue

Question 11: Youthful

Question 12: Piccolo

Question 13: Optical

Question 14: Till

BARB TEST PRACTICE QUESTIONS
SYMBOL ROTATION TEST

During the BARB test you will be required to sit the symbol rotation test. The requirement of this test is to identify which symbols are matching by rotation.

Take a look at the following 2 pairs of letters:

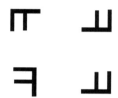

You will see that both pairs of letters are the same. The only difference is that the letters have each been rotated. Now take a look at the next 2 pairs of letters:

You will see that if each letter on the top row is rotated through all angles, it is impossible to match it up with the bottom letter directly below it.

During the symbol rotation test you will be required to identify how many pairs of symbols are **matching**. You will have to rotate the letters/symbols in your mind and decide how many of the pairs that are presented in front of you actually match. Take a look at the following 3 pairs of letters and decide how many are matching:

SAMPLE QUESTION

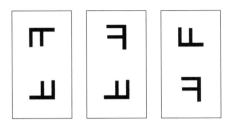

You will see that the letters in the first two boxes can be rotated to match. The pair in the third box however cannot be rotated to match. Therefore, there are **TWO** pairs in this sequence that are identical.

Now try the exercise that follows. Your task is to identify how many pairs of letters match in each sequence. You have 5 minutes to complete the exercise of 15 questions. Simply circle which answer is correct in the box beneath each question.

BARB TEST PRACTICE QUESTIONS
SYMBOL ROTATION TEST – EXERCISE 1

QUESTION 1

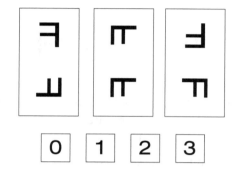

QUESTION 2

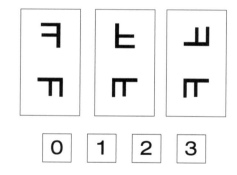

QUESTION 3

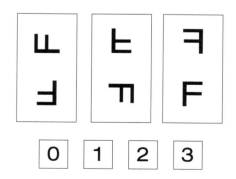

QUESTION 4

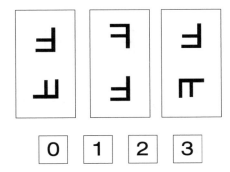

QUESTION 5

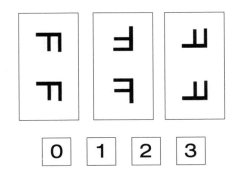

QUESTION 6

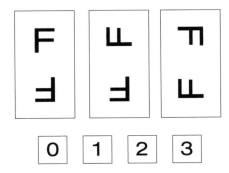

QUESTION 7

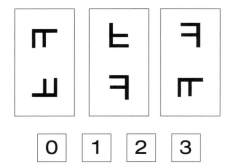

| 0 | 1 | 2 | 3 |

QUESTION 8

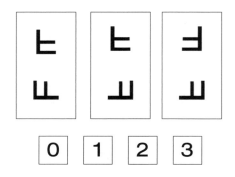

| 0 | 1 | 2 | 3 |

QUESTION 9

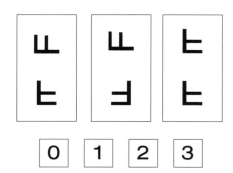

| 0 | 1 | 2 | 3 |

QUESTION 10

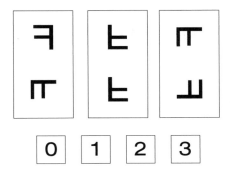

QUESTION 11

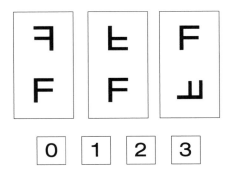

QUESTION 12

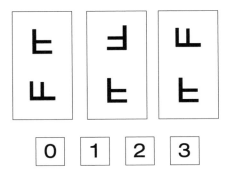

QUESTION 13

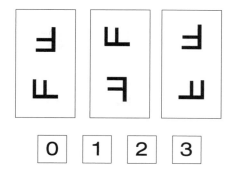

| 0 | 1 | 2 | 3 |

QUESTION 14

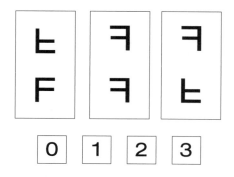

| 0 | 1 | 2 | 3 |

QUESTION 15

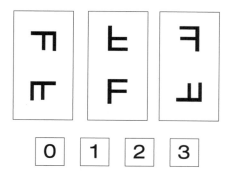

| 0 | 1 | 2 | 3 |

Now that you have completed the exercise take the time to check over your answers carefully before moving on to Symbol Rotation exercise 2.

ANSWERS TO SYMBOL ROTATION TEST - EXERCISE 1

Question 1:   3

Question 2:   2

Question 3:   1

Question 4:   0

Question 5:   2

Question 6:   3

Question 7:   3

Question 8:   1

Question 9:   2

Question 10: 3

Question 11: 0

Question 12: 0

Question 13: 1

Question 14: 2

Question 15: 1

BARB TEST PRACTICE QUESTIONS
SYMBOL ROTATION TEST – EXERCISE 2

Once again there are 15 questions during this exercise and you have 5 minutes in which to answer them. Circle the correct answer in the box provided.

QUESTION 1

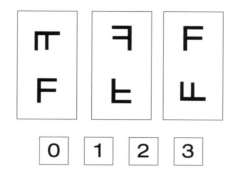

QUESTION 2

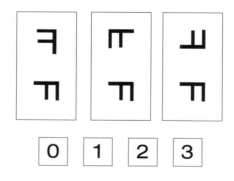

QUESTION 3

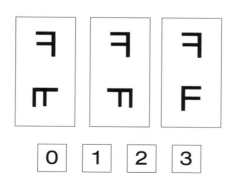

QUESTION 4

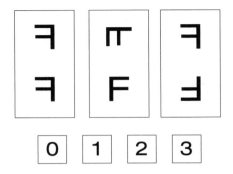

QUESTION 5

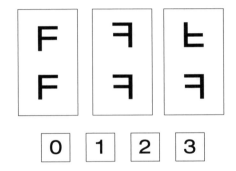

QUESTION 6

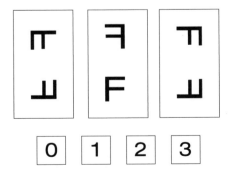

QUESTION 7

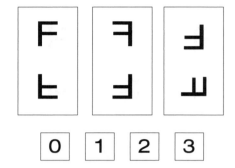

| 0 | 1 | 2 | 3 |

QUESTION 8

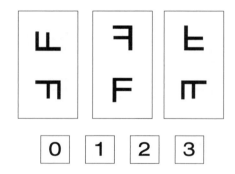

| 0 | 1 | 2 | 3 |

QUESTION 9

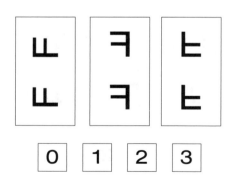

| 0 | 1 | 2 | 3 |

QUESTION 10

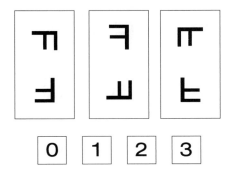

QUESTION 11

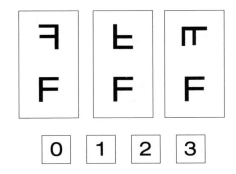

QUESTION 12

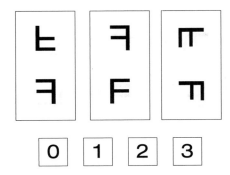

QUESTION 13

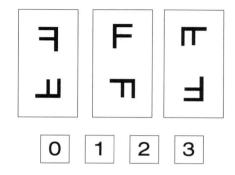

| 0 | 1 | 2 | 3 |

QUESTION 14

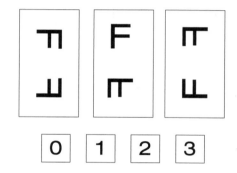

| 0 | 1 | 2 | 3 |

QUESTION 15

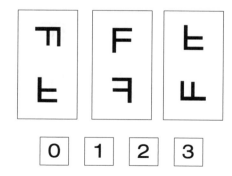

| 0 | 1 | 2 | 3 |

Now that you have completed the exercise take the time to check over your answers carefully before moving onto the next section of the guide.

ANSWERS TO SYMBOL ROTATION TEST - EXERCISE 2

Question 1:   2

Question 2:   0

Question 3:   1

Question 4:   1

Question 5:   3

Question 6:   1

Question 7:   0

Question 8:   2

Question 9:   3

Question 10: 3

Question 11: 0

Question 12: 1

Question 13: 2

Question 14: 0

Question 15: 0

CHAPTER 3
THE ROYAL NAVY RECRUITING TEST

The main purpose of the Royal Navy Recruiting Test is to establish how effective you are at figuring out problems, how good you are at English and Mathematics, and if you understand basic mechanical concepts. The vast majority of roles within the Royal Navy have some form of 'practical' element. Therefore the need to assess your mechanical reasoning ability is crucial.

The Royal Navy Recruiting Test consists of the following elements:

- A reasoning test (30 questions to be completed in 9 minutes)

- A verbal ability test (30 questions to be completed in 9 minutes)

- A numeracy test (30 questions to be completed in 16 minutes)

- A mechanical reasoning test (30 questions to be completed in 10 minutes)

During the Royal Navy Recruiting Test you will be required to sit a reasoning test. During the test you will have 9 minutes in which to answer 30 questions. Some of the questions are similar to the ones that are contained within the BARB test section of the guide. However, Royal Navy tests are generally harder to answer than the tests for the Army.

An example of a Royal Navy reasoning test question is as follows:

SAMPLE QUESTION NUMBER 1

Bill is heavier than Charlie. Who is the lightest?

The answer in this case would be Charlie as the statement indicates that Bill is heavier than Charlie, so therefore Charlie is the lighter of the two.

Answer: Charlie

Here is another example:

SAMPLE QUESTION NUMBER 2

Graham has more money than Mark. Who is the least wealthy?

The answer in this case would be Mark. The statement indicates that Graham has more money than Mark, therefore implying that Mark has less money.

Answer: Mark

When you are answering this type of question it is important that you READ the question very carefully. The questions are relatively simple but they can catch you out if you do not read them properly. Now take a look at another example:

SAMPLE QUESTION NUMBER 3

Rubbish is to bin as bread is to?

A. Breadbin
B. Knife
C. Buy
D. Wheat
E. Slice

The answer is A – Breadbin. This is because rubbish goes in the bin and bread goes in the breadbin.

Now try the Royal Navy Recruiting Test sample exercises that are provided over the next few chapters.

ROYAL NAVY RECRUITING TEST PRACTICE QUESTIONS
REASONING TEST - EXERCISE 1

During exercise 1 there are 20 sample test questions. Allow yourself 5 minutes to complete the exercise. Once you have finished the exercise, take a look at the answers and see how well you performed.

QUESTION 1

Peter works twice as long as Fred.

Who works for the least amount of time?

Answer [   ]

QUESTION 2

Victor spends less time in the shower than Rebecca.

Who is in the shower for the longest period of time?

Answer [   ]

QUESTION 3

Hillary runs a shorter distance than Beatrice.

Who runs the least distance?

Answer [   ]

QUESTION 4

Table is to sit as bed is to?

Sleep

Tired

Lie

Make

Answer [   ]

QUESTION 5

Fish is to pond as cloud is to?

Fluffy

Sky

White

Obscure

Answer [   ]

QUESTION 6

Test is to assess as shield is to?

Harm

Heavy

Protect

Hit

Answer [   ]

QUESTION 7

Make-up is to face as Shoe is to?

Wear

Tread

Lace

Foot

Answer [   ]

QUESTION 8

Carl sleeps for 7 hours and Sally sleeps for 430 minutes.

Who sleeps for the least amount of time?

Answer [   ]

QUESTION 9

Tess works for 5 hours and 45 minutes and Abdullah works for 360 minutes.

Who works for the longest period of time?

Answer [   ]

QUESTION 10

Mirror is to reflect as sun is to?

Shine

Hot

Baking

Bright

Answer [   ]

QUESTION 11

Bicycle is to ride as car is to?

Fast

Speed

Drive

Steer

Answer [   ]

QUESTION 12

Cart is to horse as Trailer is to?

Wheels

Pull

Van

Metal

Answer

QUESTION 13

Teach is to educate as talk is to?

Communicate

Speak

Shout

Whisper

Answer

QUESTION 14

Joe eats faster than Jill.

Who eats the slowest?

Answer

QUESTION 15

Wes finishes the race behind Daniel.

Who finishes the race first?

Answer

QUESTION 16

Ball is to kick as dice is to?

A. Hold   B. Win   C. Roll   D. Carry   E. Play

Answer [   ]

QUESTION 17

If the following words were arranged in alphabetical order, which one would come second?

A. Belated   B. Belief   C. Beaten   D. Beer   E. Bewildered

Answer [   ]

QUESTION 18

If the following words were arranged in alphabetical order, which one would come last?

A. Desolate   B. Desire   C. Decent   D. Delectable   E. Demented

Answer [   ]

QUESTION 19

Which of the following words contains the most vowels?

A. Tenacious   B. Collaborate   C. Between   D. Audaciously

Answer [   ]

QUESTION 20

Which of the following words contains the least vowels?

A. Barbeque   B. Tentative   C. Burlesque   D. Eaten   E. April

Answer [   ]

ANSWERS TO REASONING EXERCISE 1

1. Fred

2. Rebecca

3. Hillary

4. Lie

5. Sky

6. Protect

7. Foot

8. Carl

9. Abdullah

10. Shine

11. Drive

12. Van

13. Communicate

14. Jill

15. Daniel

16. C

17. D

18. A

19. D

20. E

ROYAL NAVY RECRUITING TEST PRACTICE QUESTIONS
REASONING TEST - EXERCISE 2

During the Royal Navy Recruiting Test you will find that the reasoning exercise may contain questions in diagrammatic format. Take a look at the following sample question.

SAMPLE QUESTION 1

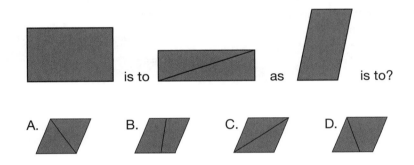

You will notice in the question that the straight line runs diagonally from the bottom left hand corner of the rectangle to the top right hand corner. The rectangle is also smaller in size than its predecessor. Therefore, the correct answer to the question is C, as the straight line runs the same through the shape, and it too is slightly smaller in size.

Take a look at the next question.

SAMPLE QUESTION 2

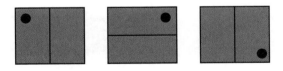

Which of the following shapes comes next in the sequence?

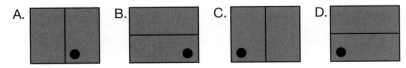

The correct answer is D. You will notice in the sample question that the black dot is moving around the shapes in a clockwise manner. In addition to this the line that runs through the shape is alternating from vertical to horizontal. The black dot starts off in the top left hand corner of the first shape. Then it progresses to the top right hand corner of the second shape before moving round to the bottom right hand corner of the third shape. Therefore D, where the black dot is in the bottom left hand corner of the shape with the horizontal line is the correct answer.

Now try Reasoning Exercise 2 which contains sample diagrammatic test questions. You have 20 minutes in which to answer 20 questions.

ROYAL NAVY RECRUITING TEST PRACTICE QUESTIONS
REASONING TEST - EXERCISE 2

QUESTION 1

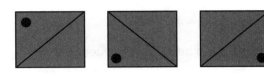

Which of the following shapes comes next in the sequence?

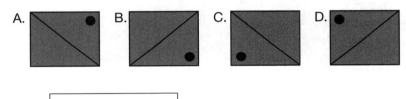

Answer

QUESTION 2

Which of the following shapes comes next in the sequence?

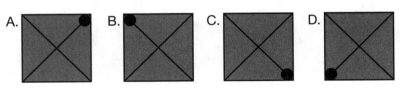

Answer

QUESTION 3

Which of the following shapes comes next in the sequence?

A.   B.   C.   D.

Answer

QUESTION 4

 is to as is to?

A.   B.   C.   D.

Answer

QUESTION 5

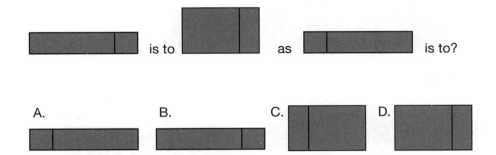

Answer [   ]

QUESTION 6

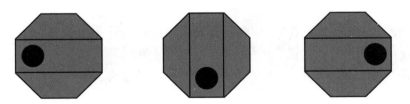

Which of the following shapes comes next in the sequence?

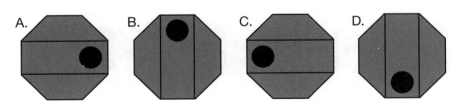

Answer [   ]

QUESTION 7

Which of the following shapes comes next in the sequence?

A.   B.   C.   D.

E. None of these

Answer

QUESTION 8

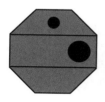 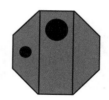 

Which of the following shapes comes next in the sequence?

A. 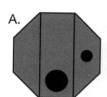   B. 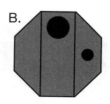   C. 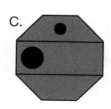   D.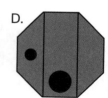

E. None of these

Answer

QUESTION 9

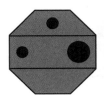 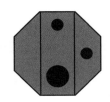 

Which of the following shapes comes next in the sequence?

A. 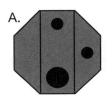   B. 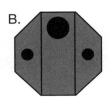   C. 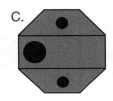   D.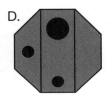

E. None of these

Answer [   ]

QUESTION 10

 is to as  is to?

A.    B.   C.    D.

E. None of these

Answer [   ]

QUESTION 11

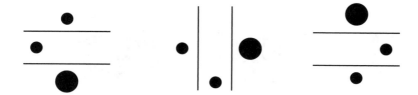

Which of the following shapes comes next in the sequence?

A.   B.   C.   D.

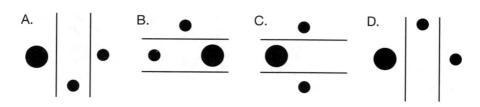

Answer [   ]

QUESTION 12

Which of the following shapes comes next in the sequence?

A.   B.   C.   D.

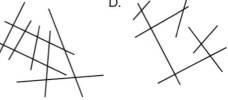

Answer [   ]

QUESTION 13

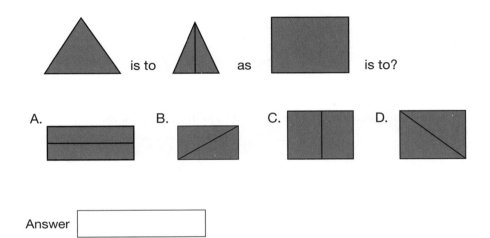

Answer

QUESTION 14

Which of the following shapes comes next in the sequence?

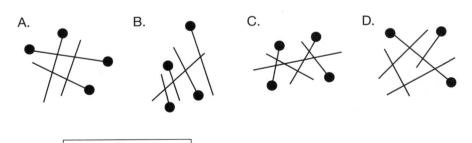

Answer

QUESTION 15

Which of the following shapes comes next in the sequence?

A.   B.  C.   D.

Answer [   ]

QUESTION 16

 is to as is to?

A.   B.   C.   D.

Answer [   ]

QUESTION 17

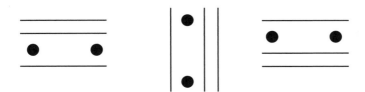

Which of the following shapes comes next in the sequence?

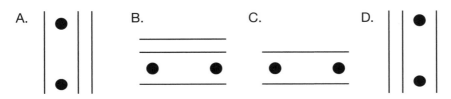

Answer

QUESTION 18

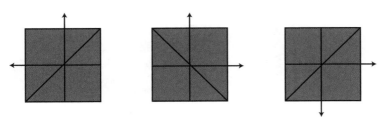

Which of the following shapes comes next in the sequence?

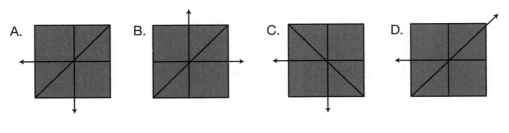

Answer

QUESTION 19

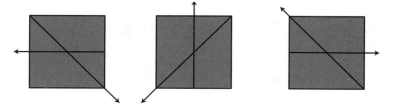

Which of the following shapes comes next in the sequence?

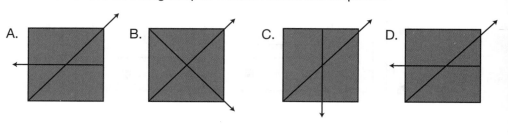

Answer

QUESTION 20

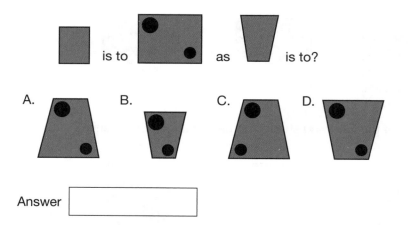

is to   as   is to?

Answer

Now that you have completed reasoning exercise 2 take the time to work through the answers, carefully checking to see which if any, you got wrong.

ANSWERS TO REASONING EXERCISE 2

1. A

2. C

3. D

4. C

5. C

6. B

7. E

8. A

9. D

10. E

11. D

12. C

13. C

14. A

15. B

16. C

17. D

18. C

19. C

20. D

ROYAL NAVY RECRUITING TEST PRACTICE QUESTIONS
REASONING TEST - EXERCISE 3

During the Royal Navy Recruiting Test you will find that the reasoning exercise may contain questions in numerical format. Take a look at the following sample question.

SAMPLE QUESTION 1

Take a look at the following row of numbers. Which number comes next from the options available?

2, 8, 14, 20, 26, 32, ?

A. 64   B. 38   C. 39   D. 42   E. 54

The answer is B – 38. The numbers are rising by 6 each time.

Now take a look at the next sample question.

SAMPLE QUESTION 2

Take a look at the following row of numbers. Which number represents '?' from the options available?

2, 2, 4, 4, 16, 6, 256, ?

A. 8   B. 512   C. 250   D. 12   E. 24

The answer is A – 8. The 1st, 3rd and 5th numbers in the row are multiples of each other. For example, 2 x 2 = 4, 4 x 4 = 16, 16 x 16 = 256. The 2nd, 4th and 6th numbers are all increasing by 2 each time. Therefore, the 8th number in the sequence will be 8.

Once you understand what is required in the test move onto the following exercise. There are 30 questions and you have a total of 9 minutes in which to answer them.

ROYAL NAVY RECRUITING TEST PRACTICE QUESTIONS
REASONING TEST - EXERCISE 3

QUESTION 1

Take a look at the following row of numbers. Which number represents '?' from the options available?

4, ?, 8, 10, 12, 14, 16

A. 3   B. 5   C. 6   D. 9   E. 18

Answer [   ]

QUESTION 2

Take a look at the following row of numbers. Which number represents '?' from the options available?

9, 10, 12, 15, 19, 24, 30, ?

A. 32   B. 34   C. 36   D. 37   E. 40

Answer [   ]

QUESTION 3

Take a look at the following row of numbers. Which number represents '?' from the options available?

11, 25, ?, 53, 67, 81, 95

A. 40   B. 42   C. 38   D. 39   E. 45

Answer [   ]

ARMED FORCES **TESTS**

QUESTION 4

Take a look at the following row of numbers. Which number comes next from the options available?

10, 10, 15, 20, 20, 30, 25, ?

A. 20   B. 25   C. 30   D. 35   E. 40

Answer [   ]

QUESTION 5

Take a look at the following row of numbers. Which number comes next from the options available?

110, 14, 95, 16, 80, 18, ?

A. 65   B. 20   C. 50   D. 55   E. 60

Answer [   ]

QUESTION 6

Take a look at the following row of numbers. Which number comes next from the options available?

76, 2, 64, 8, ?, 14, 40, 20, 28

A. 50   B. 52   C. 16   D. 42   E. 20

Answer [   ]

QUESTION 7

Take a look at the following row of numbers. Which number comes next from the options available?

50, 10, 100, 30, 200, 50, 400, 70, 800, ?

A. 90   B. 1600   C. 900   D. 100   E. 95

Answer [   ]

QUESTION 8

Take a look at the following row of numbers. Which number represents '?' from the options available?

4, 14, 23, ?, 38, 44, 49, 53

A. 27   B. 32   C. 31   D. 35   E. 34

Answer [   ]

QUESTION 9

Take a look at the following row of numbers. Which number comes next from the options available?

1, 42, 4, 38, 7, 32, 10, 24, 13, ?

A. 14   B. 15   C. 16   D. 18   E. 20

Answer [   ]

QUESTION 10

Take a look at the following row of numbers. Which number comes next from the options available?

4, 10, 7, 13, 13, 19, 22, 28, 34, ?

A. 40   B. 32   C. 54   D. 36   E. 50

Answer [   ]

QUESTION 11

Take a look at the following row of numbers. Which number comes next from the options available?

8, 10, 6, 11, 4, 12, 2, ?

A. 0   B. 1   C. 14   D. 16   E. 13

Answer [   ]

QUESTION 12

Take a look at the following row of numbers. Which two numbers in order of sequence represent '?' from the options available?

122, 112, ?, 92, 82, 72, ?

A. 110 and 62
B. 92 and 62
C. 102 and 60
D. 110 and 100
E. 102 and 62

Answer

QUESTION 13

Take a look at the following row of numbers. Which two numbers in order of sequence represent '?' from the options available?

?, 44, 36, 29, 23, 18, ?

A. 36 and 14
B. 53 and 12
C. 40 and 12
D. 38 and 14
E. 53 and 14

Answer

QUESTION 14

Take a look at the following row of numbers. Which two numbers in order of sequence represent '?' from the options available?

1, ?, 19, 28, ?, 46, 55

A. 9 and 37
B. 10 and 37
C. 9 and 36
D. 10 and 36
E. 8 and 37

Answer

QUESTION 15

Take a look at the following row of numbers. Which two numbers in order of sequence represent '?' from the options available?

134, 123, ?, 101, 90, ?, 68, 57

A. 112 and 79
B. 111 and 79
C. 112 and 81
D. 110 and 80
E. 112 and 80

Answer

QUESTION 16

Take a look at the following row of numbers. Which two numbers in order of sequence represent '?' from the options available?

?, 15, 29, 43, 57, ?, 85

A. 2 and 71
B. 1 and 72
C. 1 and 71
D. 3 and 72
E. 3 and 71

Answer

QUESTION 17

Take a look at the following row of numbers. Which two numbers in order of sequence represent '?' from the options available?

187, 20, 168, 39, 149, 58, 130, 77, ?, ?

A. 113 and 90
B. 96 and 110
C. 111 and 95
D. 112 and 96
E. 111 and 96

Answer

QUESTION 18

Take a look at the following row of numbers. Which number comes next from the options available?

5, 20, 80, ?, 1280, 5120

A. 800   B. 320   C. 640   D. 1002   E. 480

Answer [   ]

QUESTION 19

Take a look at the following row of numbers. Which number comes next from the options available?

1994, 1913, 1832, ?, 1670, 1589

A. 1750   B. 1751   C. 1752   D. 1753   E. 1754

Answer [   ]

QUESTION 20

Take a look at the following row of numbers. Which number comes next from the options available?

35, 37, 41, 47, 55, 65, ?

A. 70   B. 72   C. 74   D. 76   E. 77

Answer [   ]

Now that you've completed exercise 3, work through your answers carefully checking to see which if any, you got wrong.

ANSWERS TO REASONING EXERCISE 3

1. C - The sequence is rising by 2 each time.

2. D – Each number increases by 1 more each time. E.g. 9+1=10, 10+2=12, 12+3=15, 15+4=19 etc.

3. D – Each number increases by 14.

4. E – All odd numbers are increasing by 5 each time and all even numbers are increasing by 10.

5. A – All odd numbers are decreasing by 15 each time and all even numbers are increasing by 2.

6. B – All odd numbers are decreasing by 12 and all even numbers are increasing by 6.

7. A – All odd numbers are increasing by multiples of 2 each time. For example, 50x2=100, 100x2=200, 200x2=400 etc. All even numbers are increasing by 20 each time.

8. C – The sequence is increasing as follows:
   4+10=14, 14+9=23, 23+8+31, 31+7=38, 38+6=44, 44+5=49, 49+4=53

   You will notice that the number add each time is increases by 1.

9. A – The odd numbers are increasing by 3 each time. The even numbers decrease as follows

   42 – 4 = 38, 38 – 6 = 32, 32 – 8 = 24 etc.

   You will notice that the number subtracted each time increases by 2.

10. A – Both odd numbers and even numbers are increasing as follows:

    Odd numbers:
    4 + 3 = 7
    7 + 6 = 13
    13 + 9 = 22
    22 + 12 = 34

    Even numbers:
    10 + 3 = 13
    13 + 6 = 19
    19 + 9 = 28
    28 + 12 = 40

    You will notice that the number add each time increases by 3.

11. E – The odd numbers are decreasing 2 each time and the even numbers are increasing by 1.

12. E – The numbers are decreasing by 10 each time.

13. B – The numbers are decreasing as follows:

$$53 - 9 = 44$$
$$44 - 8 = 36$$
$$36 - 7 = 29$$
$$29 - 6 = 23$$
$$23 - 5 = 18$$
$$18 - 4 = 14$$

14. B – The numbers are increasing by 9 each time.

15. A – The numbers are decreasing by 11 each time.

16. C – The numbers are increasing by 14 each time.

17. E – The odd numbers are decreasing by 19 each time and the even numbers are increasing by 19 each time.

18. B – Each number is multiplied by 4 each time.

19. B – The numbers are decreasing by 81 each time.

20. E – The numbers are increasing each time as follows:

$$35 + 2 = 37$$
$$37 + 4 = 41$$
$$41 + 6 = 47$$
$$47 + 8 = 55$$
$$55 + 10 = 65$$
$$65 + 12 = 72$$

ROYAL NAVY RECRUITING TEST PRACTICE QUESTIONS
VERBAL ABILITY TEST

During this part of the Royal Navy Recruiting test you will be required to answer 30 questions in 9 minutes. This test is designed to assess your English language skills. The test is multiple-choice in nature and you will have 5 options to choose from. The most effective way to prepare for this type of test is to practice sample questions under timed conditions. Other ways for improving your ability include carrying out crosswords, word searches or any other tests that require an ability to work with the English language. You may also decide to purchase your own psychometric testing booklet, which can be obtained from the website www.how2become.co.uk.

Take a look at the following sample question.

SAMPLE QUESTION 1

Which of the following words is the odd one out?

A. Hammer   B. Table   C. Chisel   D. Pliers   E. Wrench

The answer is B –Table. This is because all of the other items are tools and the table is an item used for different purposes, therefore the odd one out.

Now take a look at the next sample question.

SAMPLE QUESTION 2

The following sentence has one word missing. Which word makes the best sense of the sentence?

He had been _____ for a very long time and was now starting to lose his concentration.

A. moaning   B. irritating   C. driving   D. making   E. meeting

The correct answer is C – driving, as this word makes best sense of the sentence.

Now try the following verbal ability exercise. There are 20 questions and you have 5 minutes in which to complete them.

ROYAL NAVY RECRUITING TEST PRACTICE QUESTIONS
VERBAL ABILITY TEST – EXERCISE 1

QUESTION 1

Which of the following words is the odd one out?

A. Paper   B. Pencil   C. Biro   D. Pen   E. Chalk

Answer [   ]

QUESTION 2

Which of the following is the odd one out?

A. Hut   B. Flat   C. Shed   D. House   E. Park

Answer [   ]

QUESTION 3

The following sentence has one word missing. Which word makes the best sense of the sentence?

He had spent many years in the same job and was now starting to become _____ with all of the meetings he was attending.

A. Happy   B. Caring   C. Disillusioned   D. Honourable   E. Frightened

Answer [   ]

QUESTION 4

The following sentence has two words missing. Which two words make best sense of the sentence?

The lady _____ her shopping spree at 9am and _____ finished at 4pm.

A. started / once
B. started / finally
C. wanted / eventually

D. hurried / wanted

E. commenced / really

Answer [   ]

QUESTION 5

In the line below, the word outside of the brackets will only go with three of the words inside the brackets to make longer words. Which ONE word will it NOT go with?

	A	B	C	D
In	(decent	direct	appropriate	abusive)

Answer [   ]

QUESTION 6

In the line below, the word outside of the brackets will only go with three of the words inside the brackets to make longer words. Which ONE word will it NOT go with?

	A	B	C	D
In	(coherent	dulgent	believable	candescent)

Answer [   ]

QUESTION 7

In the line below, the word outside of the brackets will only go with three of the words inside the brackets to make longer words. Which ONE word will it NOT go with?

	A	B	C	D
In	(doubtable	bred	breeding	cautiously)

Answer [   ]

QUESTION 8

Which of the following words is the odd one out?

A. Ear   B. Leg   C. Mouth   D. Nostril   E. Eye

Answer

QUESTION 9

Which of the following words is the odd one out?

A. Water   B. Lake   C. River   D. Reservoir   E. Pool

Answer

QUESTION 10

Which of the following words is the odd one out?

A. Swim   B. Run   C. Sprint   D. Sit   E. Walk

Answer

QUESTION 11

Which of the following words is the odd one out?

A. Car   B. Train   C. Trolley   D. Garage   E. Bicycle

Answer

QUESTION 12

Which of the following is the odd one out?

A. Milk   B. Tea   C. Coffee   D. Sugar   E. Spoon

Answer

QUESTION 13

The following sentence has one word missing. Which word makes the best sense of the sentence?

He wanted a football for Christmas but instead he _____ a rugby ball.

A. Given   B. Received   C. Wanted   D. Managed   E. Happy

Answer [   ]

QUESTION 14

Which two letter word can be placed in front of the following words to make a new word?

Coming   Going   Shore   Line

Answer [   ]

QUESTION 15

Which five letter word can be placed in front of the following words to make a new word?

Making   Wood   Stick   Box

Answer [   ]

QUESTION 16

The following sentence has one word missing. Which ONE word makes the best sense of the sentence?

The Captain of the aircraft informed the passengers of the _____ for turbulence.

A. Potential   B. Chance   C. Likelihood   D. Need   E. Lookout

Answer [   ]

QUESTION 17

The following sentence has one word missing. Which ONE word makes the best sense of the sentence?

He had served eight years of his sentence when he was _____ .

A. Sentenced   B. Custody   C. Released   D. Rehabilitation   E. Convict

Answer

QUESTION 18

The following sentence has two words missing. WhichTWO words make the best sense of the sentence?

Marketing strategy is a process that allows an organisation to _____ its resources on the opportunities that will allow it to _____ sales and achieve a sustainable competitive advantage.

A. concentrate / direct

B. direct / lose

C. concentrate / increase

D. process / increase

E. deliver / focus

Answer

QUESTION 19

The following sentence has one word missing. Which ONE word makes the best sense of the sentence?

A graphical chart is _____ to provide a visual display of information that would otherwise be presented in a table or text.

A. usual   B. alternatively   C. creation   D. designed   E. usually

Answer

QUESTION 20

Which of the following is the odd one out?

A. Bench   B. Stool   C. Chair   D. Sit

Answer [   ]

ANSWERS TO VERBAL ABILITY EXERCISE 1

1. A
2. E
3. C
4. B
5. D
6. C
7. A
8. B
9. A
10. D
11. D
12. E
13. B
14. On
15. Match
16. A
17. C
18. C
19. D
20. D

ROYAL NAVY/ROYAL AIR FORCE AIRMAN/AIRWOMAN TEST
MECHANICAL COMPREHENSION TEST

During the Royal Navy Recruiting test and the Royal Air Force Airman/Airwoman test you will be required to sit a mechanical comprehension test. Mechanical comprehension tests are an assessment that measures an individual's ability to learn and understand mechanical concepts. The tests are usually multiple-choice in nature and present simple, frequently encountered mechanisms and situations. The majority of mechanical comprehension tests require a working knowledge of basic mechanical operations and the application of physical laws. On the following pages I have provided you with a number of example questions to help you prepare for the tests. Work through them as quickly as possible but remember to go back and check which ones you get wrong; more importantly, make sure you understand how the correct answer is reached.

In this particular exercise there are 20 questions and you have 10 minutes in which to answer them.

QUESTION 1

Which gate is the strongest?

A

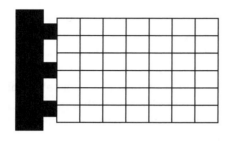

B

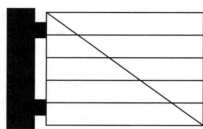

Answer

QUESTION 2

Which post is carrying the greatest load?

A. Post A

B. Post B

C. Both the same

Answer

QUESTION 3

Which direction should the wind blow in order for the plane to take off with the shortest runway?

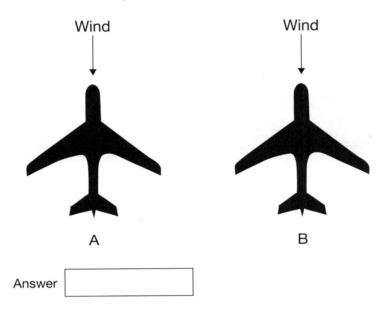

Answer

QUESTION 4

Which wheel will rotate the most number of times in 1 hour?

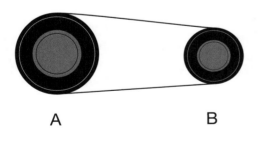

A. Wheel A

B. Wheel B

Answer

QUESTION 5

If water is poured in TUBE A until it reaches the indicated level, at what level will it reach in TUBE B?

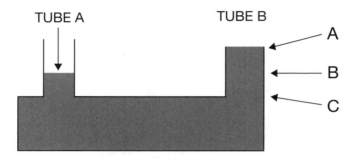

A. A

B. B

C. C

Answer

QUESTION 6

If Cog A rotates anti-clockwise at a speed of 60 rpm, at what speed and direction will Cog C rotate? (rpm = revolutions per minute)

A. 60 rpm anti-clockwise

B. 90 rpm anti-clockwise

C. 120 rpm anti-clockwise

Answer

QUESTION 7

If Cog B rotates clockwise, which way will Cog A rotate?

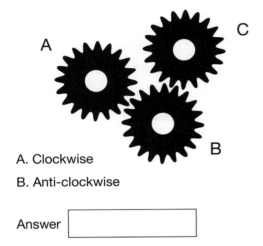

A. Clockwise

B. Anti-clockwise

Answer [   ]

QUESTION 8

How much weight in kilograms will need to be added in order to balance the beam?

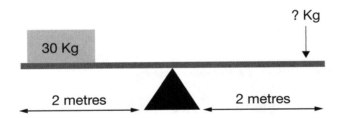

A. 10 Kg

B. 15 Kg

C. 30 Kg

D. 60 Kg

Answer [   ]

QUESTION 9

How much weight in kilograms will need to be added in order to balance the beam?

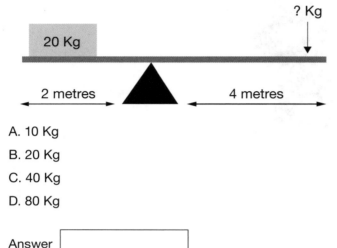

A. 10 Kg

B. 20 Kg

C. 40 Kg

D. 80 Kg

Answer

QUESTION 10

How much weight in kilograms will need to be added in order to balance the beam?

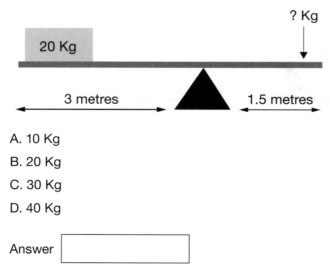

A. 10 Kg

B. 20 Kg

C. 30 Kg

D. 40 Kg

Answer

QUESTION 11

Which crane is working under the most tension?

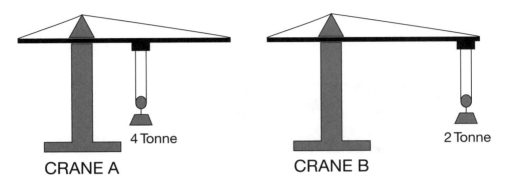

4 Tonne

CRANE A

2 Tonne

CRANE B

A. Crane A

B. Crane B

C. Both the same

Answer

QUESTION 12

Approximately how much force is required in order to lift the load?

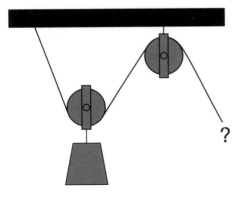

?

50 kilograms

A. 100 Kilograms

B. 50 kilograms

C. 25 Kilograms

D. 5 Kilograms

Answer

QUESTION 13

If water is poured in at Point X, which tube will overflow first?

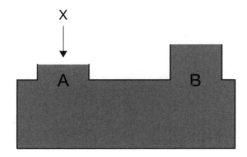

A. Tube A

B. Both at the same time

C. Tube B

Answer

QUESTION 14

Which type of beam can take the greatest load?

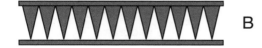

A. Beam A

B. Beam B

C. Both the same

Answer

QUESTION 15

If cog B makes 21 revolutions how many will cog A make?

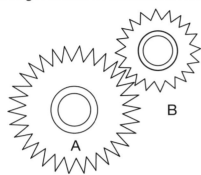

A. 7

B. 14

C. 21

D. 28

E. 42

Answer

QUESTION 16

Which load is the heaviest?

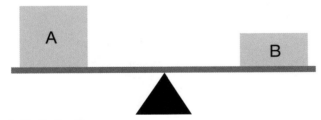

A. Both the Same

B. Load B

C. Load A

Answer

QUESTION 17

Which tank will not empty?

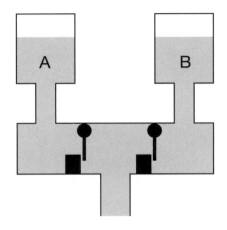

A. Tank A

B. Tank B

Answer

QUESTION 18

If cog Y moves clockwise which way will cog X move?

X

Y

A. Anti-clockwise

B. Clockwise

Answer

QUESTION 19

How much weight is required to balance the load?

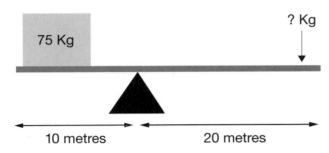

A. 37.5 Kg

B. 75 Kg

C. 125 Kg

D. 150 Kg

Answer

QUESTION 20

At which point(s) should air enter the cylinder in order to force the piston downwards?

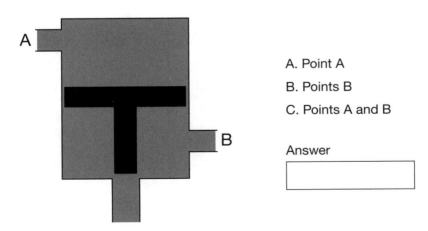

A. Point A

B. Points B

C. Points A and B

Answer

Now that you have completed mechanical comprehension exercise 1, check your answers carefully before moving onto the next section of the guide.

ANSWERS TO MECHANICAL COMPREHENSION
EXERCISE 1

1. A
2. B
3. A
4. B
5. B
6. A
7. B
8. C
9. A
10. D
11. C
12. C
13. A
14. A
15. B
16. A
17. B
18. A
19. A
20. A

ROYAL NAVY RECRUITING TEST
NUMERICAL REASONING TEST - EXERCISE 1

During the Royal Navy Recruiting Test you will also be required to sit a numerical reasoning test. The test itself consists of 30 questions and you have 16 minutes to complete it. The most effective way to prepare for the test is to carry out plenty of practice in relation to addition, subtraction, multiplication, division and also fractions, percentages and algebra.

During the real test you won't normally be permitted to use a calculator but you will be provided with a blank sheet of paper so that you can work out your answers. Within this section I have provided you with lots of sample test questions to help you prepare. There are 30 questions in this test and you have 16 minutes in which to answer them. Use a blank sheet of paper to work out the answers.

ROYAL NAVY RECRUITING TEST
NUMERICAL REASONING TEST - EXERCISE 1

QUESTION 1

58 + ? = 87

A. 26   B. 27   C. 28   D. 29   E. 30

Answer [   ]

QUESTION 2

101 - ? = 47

A. 51   B. 52   C. 53   D. 54   E. 55

Answer [   ]

QUESTION 3

? + 567 = 621

A. 51   B. 52   C. 53   D. 54   E. 65

Answer [   ]

QUESTION 4

36 x ? = 252

A. 9   B. 8   C. 7   D. 6   E. 5

Answer [   ]

QUESTION 5

8 + 9 + 9 = 13 x ?

A. 4   B. 3   C. 2   D. 1   E. 5

Answer [   ]

QUESTION 6

(46 + 28) – 4 = ? + 45

A. 36   B. 26   C. 15   D.35   E. 25

Answer [   ]

QUESTION 7

84 ÷ ? = 12 + 9

A. 2   B. 4   C. 6   D. 8   E. 3

Answer [   ]

QUESTION 8

198 - ? = 58 x 3

A. 23   B. 48   C. 42   D. 46   E. 24

Answer [   ]

QUESTION 9

100 ÷ 5 = 99 - ?

A. 19   B. 79   C. 89   D. 69   E. 29

Answer [   ]

QUESTION 10

41 x 8 = 1312 ÷ ?

A. 3   B. 4   C. 5   D. 6   E. None of these

Answer [   ]

QUESTION 11

Following the pattern shown in the number sequence below, what is the missing number?

6   18   54   ?   486   1458

A. 97   B. 302   C. 249   D. 162   E. 163

Answer [   ]

QUESTION 12

If you count from 1 to 100, how many number 5s will you pass on the way?

A. 10   B. 19   C. 11   D. 12   E. 21

Answer [   ]

QUESTION 13

50% of 842 = ?

A. 241   B. 240   C. 420   D. 402   E. 421

Answer [   ]

QUESTION 14

75% of 3300 = ?

A. 2745   B. 2475   C. 2455   D. 3000   E. 2905

Answer [   ]

QUESTION 15

80% of 800 = ?

A. 860   B. 880   C. 640   D. 600   E. 680

Answer [   ]

QUESTION 16

15% of 200 = ?

A. 45   B. 35   C. 30   D. 15   E. 7.5

Answer [   ]

QUESTION 17

45% of 500 = ?

A. 200   B. 225   C. 240   D. 245   E. 725

Answer [   ]

QUESTION 18

7% of 350 = ?

A. 24.5   B. 20.5   C. 245   D. 205   E. 25.5

Answer [   ]

QUESTION 19

9952 – 2599 = ?

A. 7535   B. 3577   C. 5733   D. 3753   E. 7353

Answer [   ]

QUESTION 20

9 x 4.5 = ?

A. 40   B. 39.5   C. 41.5   D. 40.5   E. 42

Answer [   ]

QUESTION 21

1888 ÷ 4 = ?

A. 422   B. 472   C. 247   D. 427   E. 224

Answer [   ]

QUESTION 22

8665 – 856 = ?

A. 8097   B. 7808   C. 7809   D. 8079   E. 7089

Answer [   ]

QUESTION 23

663 + 113 = ?

A. 76   B. 74   C. 775   D. 716   E. 776

Answer [   ]

QUESTION 24

A rectangle has an area of 48cm². The length of one side is 6cm. What is the perimeter of the rectangle?

A. 24 inches   B. 24cm   C. 18cm   D. 28cm   E. 28 inches

Answer [   ]

QUESTION 25

A square has a perimeter of 36cm. What is the length of one side?

A. 81cm   B. 72cm   C. 18cm   D. 81 metres   E. 9cm

Answer [   ]

QUESTION 26

During the Royal Navy Recruiting Test a candidate achieves 60%. If the maximum possible score was 80, what score did the candidate achieve?

A. 60   B. 40   C. 44   D. 48   E. 50

Answer [   ]

QUESTION 27

Is 1589 divisible by 7?

A. Yes   B. No

Answer [   ]

QUESTION 28

During the Royal Navy Recruiting Test a candidate achieves 40%. If the maximum possible score was 85, what score did the candidate achieve?

A. 34   B. 35   C. 36   D. 44   E. 45

Answer [   ]

QUESTION 29

One side of a rectangle is 15cm. If the area of the rectangle is 255cm^2, what is the length of the other side?

A. 15cm   B. 17cm   C. 6cm   D. 7cm   E. 9cm

Answer [   ]

QUESTION 30

A rectangle has an area of 144cm^2. The length of one side is 16cm. What is the perimeter?

A. 8cm   B. 16cm   C. 10cm   D. 12cm   E. None of these.

Answer [   ]

Now that you have completed the first numerical reasoning exercise, take the time to check through your answers carefully before moving onto exercise 2.

ANSWERS TO NUMERICAL REASONING EXERCISE 1

1. D	16. C
2. D	17. B
3. D	18. A
4. C	19. E
5. C	20. D
6. E	21. B
7. B	22. C
8. E	23. E
9. B	24. D
10. B	25. E
11. D	26. D
12. D	27. A
13. E	28. A
14. B	29. B
15. C	30. E

ROYAL NAVY RECRUITING TEST
NUMERICAL REASONING TEST - EXERCISE 2

There are 30 questions in this exercise and you have 16 minutes in which to answer them. Once again use a blank sheet of paper to work out the answers. You are not permitted to use a calculator.

QUESTION 1

Calculate 6.99 + 18.09

A. 25.08   B. 24.08   C. 24.80   D.25.80   E. 23.08

Answer

QUESTION 2

Calculate 13.26 – 2.22

A. 11.4   B. 11.04   C. 10.04   D. 12.04   E. 11.06

Answer

QUESTION 3

Calculate 138.22 – 12.45

A. 126.77   B. 127.77   C. 152.77   D. 127.55   E. 125.77

Answer

QUESTION 4

Calculate 4671.80 – 27.88

A. 4643.92   B. 4346.29   C. 4634.92   D. 4432.92   E. 4634.02

Answer

 THE **TESTING** SERIES

QUESTION 5

Calculate 278.09 + 325.80

A. 603.99   B. 630.89   C. 603.89   D. 503.89   E. 599.09

Answer [   ]

QUESTION 6

Calculate 17.1 − 9.8

A. 8.3   B. 6.3   C. 7.2   D. 7.6   E. 7.3

Answer [   ]

QUESTION 7

Calculate 5.6 x 2.2

A. 10.12   B. 10.62   C. 11.32   D. 12.32   E. 13.22

Answer [   ]

QUESTION 8

Calculate 5.1 x 4.7

A. 23.79   B. 23.97   C. 24.97   D. 20.7   E. 20.8

Answer [   ]

QUESTION 9

Calculate 19.8 x 3

A. 27.24   B. 59.4   C. 58.9   D. 57.4   E. 57.24

Answer [   ]

QUESTION 10

Calculate 4.4 x 4.4

A. 88.88   B. 44.44   C. 16.16   D.19.36   E. 8.44

Answer [   ]

QUESTION 11

Convert 0.75 to a fraction?

A. 1/75   B. 3/4   C. 7/5   D. 2/5   E. 4/6

Answer [   ]

QUESTION 12

Jake wants to lose 10 kilograms. After 3 months he has lost 3/4 of this amount. How much has he lost?

A. 5 kg   B. 4 kg   C. 7 kg   D. 7.5 kg   E. 8 kg

Answer [   ]

QUESTION 13

Hayley weighs 75 kilograms. If she wants to lose 8% of her total body weight, how much does she need to lose?

A. 6kg   B. 7kg   C. 8kg   D. 60kg   E. 70kg

Answer [   ]

QUESTION 14

If y = 45 and s = 965, then s – y =

A. 290   B. 92   C. 920   D. 930   E. 935

Answer [   ]

QUESTION 15

15 out of 75 hospital patients have leg injuries. What percentage of patients do not have leg injuries?

A. 60   B. 20   C. 11.25   D. 12   E. 80

Answer [   ]

QUESTION 16

Alison has been keeping a record of how much she has been withdrawing from the cash point machine. Over the last 10 weeks she has withdrawn the following amounts:

£10   £20   £80   £60   £20   £10   £90   £100   £50   £30

What percentage of her withdrawals are under £60?

A. 40%   B. 50%   C. 60%   D. 70%   E. 65%

Answer [   ]

QUESTION 17

1/5 x 2/5 = ?

A. 2/5   B. 2/25   C. 3/25   D. 4/25   E. 2/525

Answer [   ]

QUESTION 18

1/3 x 1/3 = ?

A. 1/9   B. 1/33   C. 1/3   D. 1/39   E. 3/4

Answer [   ]

QUESTION 19

1/2 ÷ 3/4 = ?

A. 2/3   B. 4/5   C. 3/4   D. 7/8   E. 3/5

Answer [   ]

QUESTION 20

What is the number 55.87244 correct to three decimal places?

A. 55.873   B. 55.87   C. 55.882   D. 55.872   E. 55.883

Answer [   ]

QUESTION 21

The clock above reads 10:10 am. How many degrees will the large (minute) hand have turned when the time reaches 11:00 am?

A. 180°   B. 250°   C. 270°   D. 300°   E. 320°

Answer

QUESTION 22

The clock above reads 10:10 am. How many degrees will the large (minute) hand have turned when the time reaches 11:30 am?

A. 360°   B. 380°   C. 400°   D. 460°   E. 480°

Answer

QUESTION 23

The clock above reads 10:10 am. How many degrees will the large (minute) hand have turned when the time reaches 11:07 am?

A. 342°   B. 340°   C. 322°   D. 312°   E. 307°

Answer

QUESTION 24

The clock above reads 10:10 am. How many degrees will the small (hour) hand have turned when the time reaches 8:10 pm?

A. 60°   B. 300°   C. 360°   D. 180°   E. 270°

Answer [   ]

QUESTION 25

The clock above reads 10:10 am. How many degrees will the small (hour) hand have turned when the time reaches 11:10 pm?

A. 305°   B. 390°   C. 360°   D. 180°   E. 270°

Answer [   ]

QUESTION 26

The clock above reads 10:10 am. How many degrees will the small (hour) hand have turned when the time reaches 13:10 pm?

A. 45°   B. 30°   C. 15°   D. 180°   E. 90°

Answer [   ]

QUESTION 27

The Fire Service reports the following number and type of fires in a 12 month period:

Car fires	100
Chimney fires	200
House fires	50
Derelict building fires	350
Rubbish fires	300

What percentage of fires were chimney fires?

A. 10%   B. 15%   C. 20%   D. 25%   E. 30%

Answer [　　　　　　　　]

QUESTION 28

The Fire Service reports the following number and type of fires in a 12 month period:

Car fires	200
Chimney fires	100
House fires	350
Derelict building fires	150
Rubbish fires	200

What percentage of fires were derelict building fires?

A. 10%   B. 15%   C. 20%   D. 25%   E. 30%

QUESTION 29

1200 x 0.4 = ?

A. 560   B. 440   C. 990   D. 330   E. 480

Answer [　　　　　　　　]

QUESTION 30

760 x 0.2 = ?

A. 125   B. 122   C. 152   D. 142   E. 150

Answer [   ]

Now that you have completed numerical reasoning exercise 2 take the time to carefully work through your answers before moving onto the next section of the guide.

ANSWERS TO NUMERICAL REASONING TEST
EXERCISE 2

1. A
2. B
3. E
4. A
5. C
6. E
7. D
8. B
9. B
10. D
11. B
12. D
13. A
14. C
15. E

16. C
17. B
18. A
19. A
20. D
21. D
22. E
23. A
24. B
25. B
26. E
27. C
28. B
29. E
30. C

CHAPTER 4

THE ROYAL AIR FORCE AIRMAN/AIRWOMAN SELECTION TEST

Before we get into some sample practice questions for the Royal Air Force Selection Test (AST), let's first recap on what the test actually involves.

The AST consists of a number of different aptitude tests, which are designed to assess which careers in the RAF you are most suited to. There are many different career opportunities available and each one requires a different level of skill. The AST consists of seven timed multiple choice aptitude tests as follows:

> A verbal reasoning test which assesses how well you can interpret written information. During this test you will have 15 minutes to answer 20 questions;

> A numerical reasoning test which determines how accurately you can interpret numerical information such as charts, graphs and tables. The test will also assess your ability to use fractions, decimals and different formula. There are two parts to this test. During the first test you will have just 4 minutes to answer 12 questions that are based on fractions, decimals and formula. During the second test you will have 11 minutes to answer 15 questions that relate to different graphs and tables;

> A work rate test which is used to assess how quickly and accurately you can carry out routine tasks. During this test you will have 4 minutes to answer 20 questions;

> A spatial reasoning test designed to examine your ability to work with different shapes and objects. During this test you will have just 4 minutes to answer 10 questions;

> A mechanical comprehension test which is used to assess how effectively you can work with different mechanical concepts. During this particular test you will have 10 minutes in which to answer 20 questions;

> An electrical comprehension test which will assess your ability to work with different electrical concepts. During this test you will have 11 minutes to complete 21 questions.

> A memory test which determines how accurately you can remember and recall information. There are two parts to this test and you will have a total of 10 minutes in which to answer 20 questions.

Now that you understand what the test involves, let's move onto some sample test questions. Please note: sample Mechanical Comprehension Test questions for the AST are contained within the Royal Navy Recruiting Test section of this guide.

ROYAL AIR FORCE AIRMAN/AIRWOMAN TEST
VERBAL REASONING TEST - EXERCISE 1

Read the following information carefully before answering the questions that follow. You have 5 minutes to complete exercise 1

Car A is black in colour and has 4 months left on the current MOT. The tax is due in 8 months time. The car has no service history and has completed 46,500 miles. The car has had 2 owners.

Car B is red in colour and has a full 12 months MOT. The tax is not due for another 8 months. The car has completed 14,459 miles and has only had 1 owner. There is a full service history with the car.

Car C has no tax. The MOT is due to run out in 3 months time and the car has no service history. The speedometer reading is 121,000 miles and the car, which is black in colour, has had a total of 8 owners.

Car D is black in colour and has 7 months left on the current MOT. The tax is due in 8 months time. The car has no service history and has completed 43,000 miles. The car has had 2 owners.

Car E has 5 months tax. The MOT runs out in 7 months time. The car, which is the colour red has a partial service history and has completed 87,000 miles. It has had a total of 3 owners.

QUESTION 1

You want a car that is red in colour and has a full service history with less than 100,000 miles. Which car would you choose?

A. Car A   B. Car B   C. Car C   D. Car E   E. None of these

Answer [   ]

QUESTION 2

You want a car that has more than 6 months tax. You are not concerned about the colour but you do want 12 months MOT. Which car would you choose?

A. Car A   B. Car B   C. Car C   D. Car D   E. Car E

Answer [   ]

QUESTION 3

You want a car that is black in colour and has had no more than 4 owners. You want a minimum of 6 months tax. The mileage is irrelevant but you do want at least 7 months MOT. Which car would you choose?

A. Car A   B. Car B   C. Car C   D. Car D   E. Car E

Answer [   ]

ROYAL AIR FORCE AIRMAN/AIRWOMAN TEST
VERBAL REASONING TEST - EXERCISE 2

Read the following information carefully before answering the questions that follow. You have 5 minutes to complete exercise 2

FLIGHT A, outbound, leaves at 10am and arrives at 2pm. The cost of the flight is £47 but this does not include a meal or refreshments. The return flight departs at 5am and arrives at its destination at 9am.

FLIGHT B, outbound, leaves at 1pm and arrives at 5pm. The cost of the flight is £89 and this includes a meal and refreshments. The return flight departs at 6pm and arrives at its destination at 11pm.

FLIGHT C, outbound, leaves at 6pm and arrives at 10:55pm. The cost of the flight is £69 but this does not include a meal or refreshments. The return flight departs at 10am and arrives at its destination at 3pm.

FLIGHT D, outbound, leaves at midnight and arrives at 6am. The cost of the flight is £175, which does include a meal and refreshments. The return flight departs at 2pm and arrives at 8pm.

FLIGHT E, outbound, leaves at 12noon and arrives at 1:45pm. The cost of the flight is £45, which does not include a meal and refreshments. The return flight departs at 5pm and arrives at its destination at 7pm.

QUESTION 1

You want a flight where the outbound flight arrives before 2pm on the day of departure. You don't want to pay any more than £50. Which flight would you choose?

A. Flight A   B. Flight B   C. Flight C   D. Flight D   E. Flight E

Answer [   ]

QUESTION 2

You don't want to pay more than £100 for the flight. You want a meal and the outbound departure time must be in the afternoon. Which flight would you choose?

A. Flight A   B. Flight B   C. Flight C   D. Flight D   E. Flight E

Answer [   ]

QUESTION 3

You want an outbound flight that departs in the afternoon between 12noon and 6pm. The cost of the flight must be below £100 and you do want a meal. The return flight must arrive at your destination before 6pm. Which flight would you choose?

A. Flight A   B. Flight B   C. Flight C   D. Flight D   E. None of these

Answer [   ]

ROYAL AIR FORCE AIRMAN/AIRWOMAN TEST
VERBAL REASONING TEST - EXERCISE 3

Read the following information carefully before answering the questions that follow. You have 5 minutes to complete exercise 3

Marcus and Sally live in the town of Graysham. They have been married for 17 years and have two children. Tony lives on his own 3 miles away in the village of Harmet. Derek and Barbara live just down the road from Tony in the town of Twinfort with their three children. Marcus and Derek work together as electrical engineers whilst Tony works in the local village shop. Marcus and Sally's children go to the same school as one of Derek and Barbara's children. Derek and Barbara's remaining two children go to school in the town of Gillwingham.

QUESTION 1

Which one of the following statements is definitely true?

A. Tony is married to Barbara

B. Tony lives in Twinfort

C. Twinfort is a village

D. Derek and Barbara's children all go to the same school

E. Tony lives 3 miles away from Marcus and Sally

Answer [   ]

QUESTION 2

Two of Derek and Barbara's children go to the same school as Marcus and Sally's children?

A. True   B. False   C. Cannot say

Answer [   ]

QUESTION 3

Tony lives on his own 3 miles away from Derek and Barbara in the village of Harmet.

A. True   B. False   C. Cannot say

Answer [   ]

ANSWERS TO ROYAL AIR FORCE
VERBAL REASONING TESTS

Verbal Reasoning test 1

1. B

2. B

3. D

Verbal Reasoning test 2

1. E

2. B

3. E

Verbal Reasoning test 3

1. E

2. B

3. C

ROYAL AIR FORCE AIRMAN/AIRWOMAN TEST
NUMERICAL REASONING TEST

During the Airman/Airwoman Selection Test you will be required to undertake a numerical reasoning test. This test is used to determine how accurately you can interpret numerical information such as charts, graphs and tables. The test will also assess your ability to use fractions, decimals and different formula. As you can imagine, the most effective way to prepare for this type of test is to carry out lots of sample numerical reasoning test questions, without the aid of a calculator.

During the actual numerical reasoning test with the RAF you will have a specific amount of time to answer each question. It is important that you do not spend too much time on one particular question. Remember that the clock is ticking. Have a go at the first numerical reasoning exercise that now follows and use a blank sheet of paper to work out your calculations. Remember to check your answers very carefully. It is important that you check any incorrect answers to see why you got them wrong.

You have 10 minutes in which to answer the 20 questions. Calculators are not permitted.

ROYAL AIR FORCE AIRMAN/AIRWOMAN TEST
NUMERICAL REASONING TEST - EXERCISE 1

QUESTION 1

5.2 x 1.7 =

A. 7.85   B. 8.85   C. 8.84   D. 7.84   E. 7.86

Answer

QUESTION 2

8.8 x 5.6 =

A. 47.82   B. 40.48   C. 49.82   D. 48.29   E. 49.28

Answer

QUESTION 3

4.4 ÷ 2.2 =

A. 2   B. 1.2   C. 6.8   D. 2.4   E. 8.8

Answer

QUESTION 4

6.2 x 2.1 =

A. 13. 21   B. 12.30   C. 13.03   D. 13.02   E. 13.20

Answer

QUESTION 5

554.12 + 330.61 =

A. 884.3   B. 884.37   C. 887.73   D. 884.73   E. 868.74

Answer [   ]

QUESTION 6

Which of the following is not a fraction equivalent to 3/4?

A. 7/10

B. 9/12

C. 12/16

D. 21/28

E. 30/40

Answer [   ]

QUESTION 7

Which of the following is not a fraction equivalent to 6/8?

A. 48/64

B. 12/16

C. 18/24

D. 3/4

E. 22/32

Answer [   ]

QUESTION 8

Which of the following is not a fraction equivalent to 5/7?

A. 30/42

B. 15/21

C. 10/15

D. 20/28

E. 25/35

Answer

QUESTION 9

3/4 + 7/7 =

A. 1 3/4   B. 1 4/5   C. 1 8/9   D. 2 3/4   E. 1 7/8

Answer

QUESTION 10

6/8 + 5/10 =

A. 1 3/4   B. 1 4/5   C. 1 1/2   D. 1 1/4   E. 1 7/8

Answer

QUESTION 11

What is the following as a decimal?

One and Two Hundredths

A. 1.002   B. 1.02   C. 1.2

Answer

QUESTION 12

What is 71/100 as a decimal?

A. 71.0   B. 7.1   C. 0.71   D. 0.071   E. 0.0071

Answer [   ]

QUESTION 13

What is 31/50 as a decimal?

A. 31.5   B. 0.62   C. 0.315   D. 31.2   E. 62.0

Answer [   ]

QUESTION 14

In the following question what is the value of t?

$$\frac{5t - 20}{5} = 2$$

A. 2   B. 30   C. 15   D. 20   E. 6

Answer [   ]

QUESTION 15

$$\frac{6t - 42}{2} = 15$$

A. 10   B. 11   C. 72   D. 14   E. 12

Answer [   ]

QUESTION 16

18.4 x 12.8 =

A. 31.2   B. 253   C. 235   D. 235.5   E. 235.52

Answer

QUESTION 17

12.6 ÷ 3 =

A. 4.2   B. 4.1   C. 3.2   D. 3.1   E. 37.8

Answer

QUESTION 18

42.2 ÷ 5 =

A. 8.42   B. 8.44   C. 8.40   D. 4.44   E. 4.42

Answer

QUESTION 19

16.8 x 7.1 =

A. 119.28   B. 119.82   C. 142.7   D. 112.9   E. 119.8

Answer

QUESTION 20

50.2 x 3.3 =

A. 164.46   B. 165.56   C. 166.66   D.165.66   E. 166.65

Answer

Now check your answers to see which if any, you got wrong. Once you are satisfied, move on to the next numerical exercise.

ANSWERS TO NUMERICAL REASONING TEST
EXERCISE 1

1. C
2. E
3. A
4. D
5. D
6. A
7. E
8. C
9. A
10. D
11. B
12. C
13. B
14. E
15. E
16. E
17. A
18. B
19. A
20. D

ROYAL AIR FORCE AIRMAN/AIRWOMAN TEST
NUMERICAL REASONING TEST - EXERCISE 2

On the following pages I have supplied you with a number of sample numerical reasoning tests which will improve your ability to use tables and graphs. Allow yourself 10 minutes to answer the 9 questions.

ROYAL AIR FORCE AIRMAN/AIRWOMAN TEST
NUMERICAL REASONING TEST - EXERCISE 2

Look at Table 1 below and then answer the questions that follow.

TABLE 1. The following table lists the type of bonus each member of staff will receive if they reach a specific number of sales per hour they work. The table has not yet been completed. Staff work seven hour shifts. In order to answer the questions you will need to complete the table.

TIME	10 sales	20 sales	30 sales	40 sales
1st hour	£23.50	£27.50	£35.95	£42.60
2nd hour	£20.00	£23.50	-	£36.35
3rd hour	£16.50	-	£25.55	-
4th hour	£13.00	£15.50	£20.35	-
5th hour	£9.50	-	£15.15	£17.60
6th hour	-	£7.50	£9.95	£11.35
7th hour	£2.50	£3.50	-	£5.10

Note: If a worker achieves 180 sales or more during their 7 hour shift they will receive an additional £50 bonus.

QUESTION 1

If the table was complete how much could a worker earn in bonuses if they reached 10 sales every hour of their 7 hour shift?

A. £99.50   B. £98.50   C. £101   D. £100.50   E. £91

Answer [   ]

QUESTION 2

How much would a worker earn in bonuses if they reached 20 sales per hour for the first 4 hours of their shift and 40 sales per hour for the remaining 3 hours of their shift?

A. £170.05   B. £112.10   C. £120.05   D. £121.20   E. £121.10

Answer [   ]

QUESTION 3

How much would a worker earn in bonuses if they reached 10 sales during their first and last hour, 20 sales during the 2nd and 6th hours, 30 sales during the 3rd and 5th hours and 40 sales during the 4th hour?

A. £124.50   B. £124   C. £121.55   D. £125.50   E. £125.55

Answer [   ]

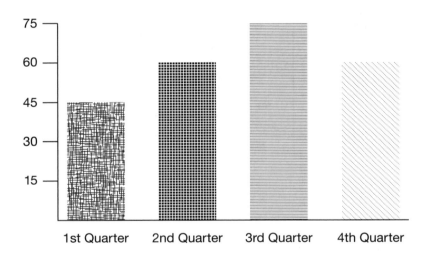

The above chart indicates the total number of day's sickness taken per quarter at the Arlingford Car Depot. Study the graph and answer the questions.

QUESTION 4

How many days sickness were taken in total during the year?

A. 220   B. 200   C. 120   D. 2400   E. 240

Answer [   ]

QUESTION 5

What was the average number of days sickness taken per quarter?

A. 240   B. 40   C. 50   D. 60   E. 80

Answer [   ]

QUESTION 6

If the total number of sickness days reduced the following year by 40%, what would the total be?

A. 144   B. 96   C. 80   D. 775   E. 190

Answer [   ]

The following graph indicates the total monthly profits of four competing companies during a 5 month period. Study the graph and answer the questions that follow.

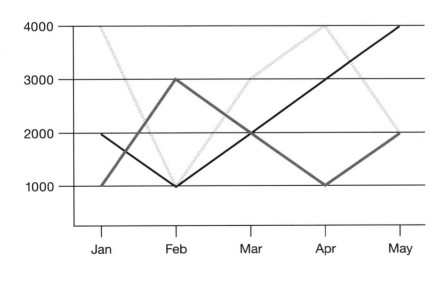

.... Company A

▬▬▬▬ Company B

———— Company C

QUESTION 7

Over the 5 month period, which company(s) made the greatest profit?

A. Company A   B. Company B   C. Company C   D. Companies A and B

Answer

QUESTION 8

What were the total combined profits for all three companies over the 5 month period?

A. 25000   B. 35000   C. 27000   D. 32000   E. 30000

Answer

QUESTION 9

During which month was the average profit across the three companies the lowest?

A. January   B. February   C. March   D. April   E. May

Answer

Now check your answers before moving on to the next section of the guide.

ANSWERS TO NUMERIAL REASONING TEST
EXERCISE 2

1. E

2. A

3. C

4. E

5. D

6. A

7. A

8. B

9. B

ROYAL AIR FORCE AIRMAN/AIRWOMAN TEST
WORK RATE TEST

During the AST you will be required to undertake a work rate test. This form of test assesses your ability to work quickly and accurately whilst carrying out routine tasks; something which is integral to the role of an Airman/Airwoman.

Before we move on to the test questions, let's take a look at a sample question. To begin with, study the following box which contains different numbers, letters and symbols.

5	6	3	1	2	NUMBERS
J	F	T	S	W	LETTERS
◣	✚	☾	⬠	●	SYMBOLS

COLUMNS

In the sample questions that I have provided you with, you will be given a code consisting of numbers, letters or symbols. Your task is to look at the 5 provided alternative codes and decide which one has been taken from the SAME columns as the original code.

For example, take a look at the following code:

CODE A – 563

Now look at the 5 alternatives, which are taken from the above grid and decide which code has been taken from the same columns as code A.

A. J ☾ 2   B. ◣ FT   C. ✚ 51   D. ● 6S   E. 3J2

You can see that the answer is in fact B and the code ◣ FT. The reason for this is that the code has been taken from the **same columns** as the original code of **563**.

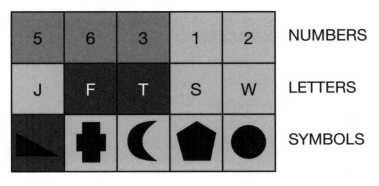

NUMBERS

LETTERS

SYMBOLS

COLUMNS

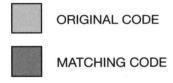

ORIGINAL CODE

MATCHING CODE

Now take the time to work through the following exercise. You have 10 minutes in which to work through the 10 questions.

ROYAL AIR FORCE AIRMAN/AIRWOMAN TEST
WORK RATE TEST - EXERCISE 1

QUESTION 1

Which of the answers below is an alternative to the code **281**?

8	7	1	2
■	◆	●	◣
S	E	T	H

A. 8■E   **B.** HS●   **C.** ◣5◆   **D.** T■H

Answer [   ]

QUESTION 2

Which of the answers below is an alternative to the code **493**?

4	2	9	3
◆	■	◣	●
D	A	Q	X

A. D◣X   **B.** ◆QA   **C.** ◣AD   **D.** DAX

Answer [   ]

QUESTION 3

Which of the answers below is an alternative to the code **987**?

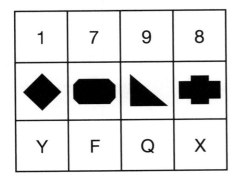

Answer [   ]

QUESTION 4

Which of the answers below is an alternative to the code **135**?

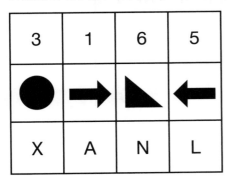

Answer [   ]

QUESTION 5

Which of the answers below is an alternative to the code **1WR**?

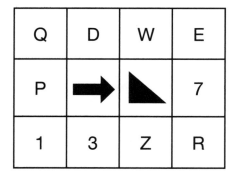

A. PZE   **B.** ◣ 17   **C.** ➡1R   **D.** Q3R

Answer [   ]

QUESTION 6

Which of the answers below is an alternative to the code **DAE**?

A	Q	R	E
1	⬅	✚	6
↰	D	7	↳

A. Q17   **B.** ↰Q6   **C.** ⬅16   **D.** ERA

Answer [   ]

QUESTION 7

Which of the answers below is an alternative to the code **326**?

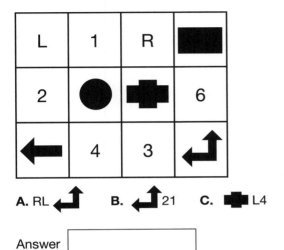

A. RL   **B.** 21 **C.** L4 **D.** R62

Answer [   ]

QUESTION 8

Which of the answers below is an alternative to the code **£4&**?

L	1	R	£
2	9	&	6
=	4	3	>

A. 61> **B.** >9= **C.** >1R **D.** =13

Answer [   ]

QUESTION 9

Which of the answers below is an alternative to the code **Q3%**?

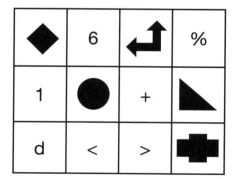

A. 1&

B. 13&

C. t 1

D. 11&

Answer

QUESTION 10

Which of the answers below is an alternative to the code **1>6**?

A. +d<

B. d+<

C. d<

D. 1>%

Answer

ANSWERS TO WORK RATE TEST EXERCISE 1

1. B
2. A
3. D
4. C
5. A
6. C
7. A
8. C
9. A
10. B

ROYAL AIR FORCE AIRMAN/AIRWOMAN TEST
SPATIAL REASONING TEST

During the Airman/Airwoman Selection Test you will be required to undertake a spatial reasoning test.

The definition of spatial reasoning is as follows:

'The ability to interpret and make drawings from mental images and visualise movement or change in those images.'

During the AST you will be confronted with a number of spatial reasoning questions and the only effective way to prepare for them is to try as many as you can in the build up to the actual test. Let's now take a look at a sample question.

SAMPLE QUESTION

Take a look at the following 3 shapes. Note the letters on the side of each shape:

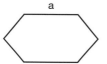 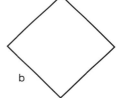

Join all of the 3 shapes together with the corresponding letters to make the following shape:

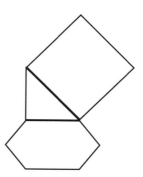

During the spatial reasoning exercise that now follows your task is to look at the given shapes and decide which of the examples matches the shape when joined together by the corresponding letters. You have 3 minutes to answer the 8 questions.

ROYAL AIR FORCE AIRMAN/AIRWOMAN TEST
SPATIAL REASONING TEST - EXERCISE 1

QUESTION 1

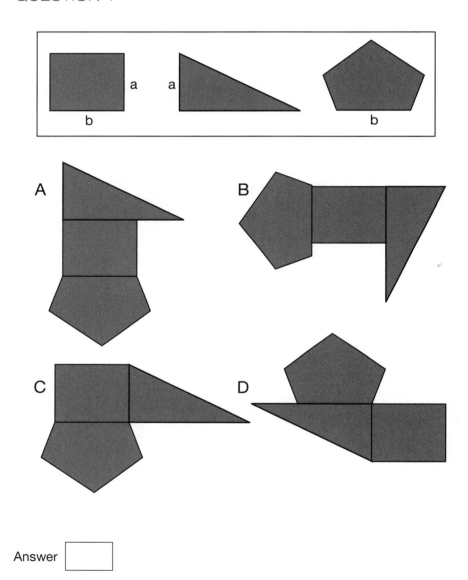

Answer [   ]

QUESTION 2

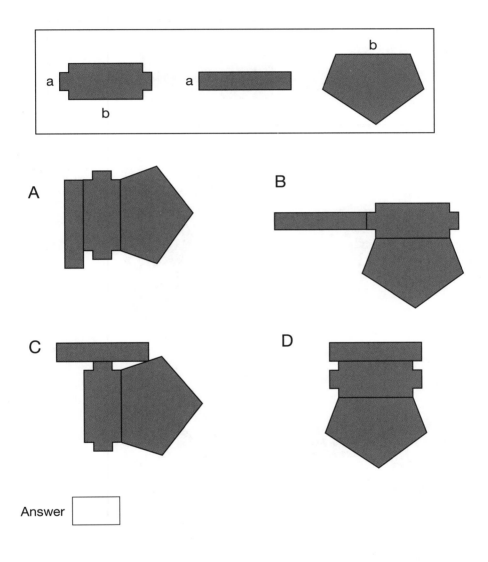

Answer [   ]

QUESTION 3

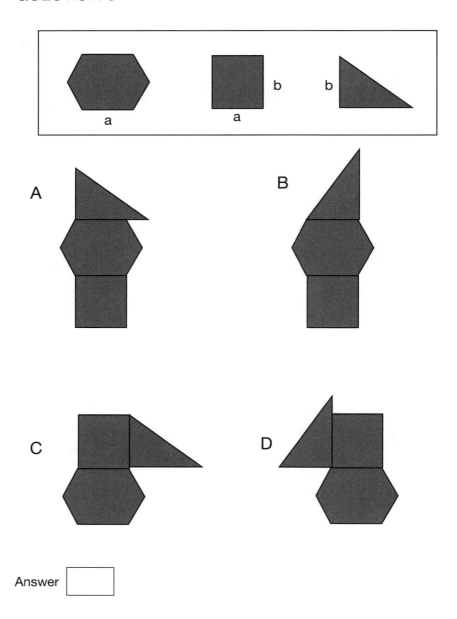

Answer

QUESTION 4

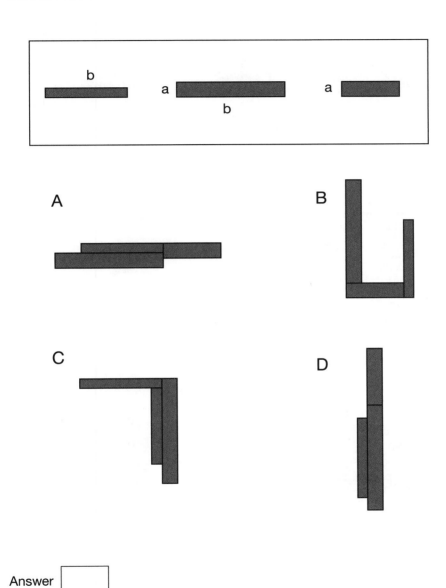

Answer ☐

QUESTION 5

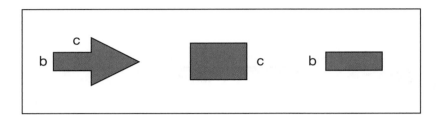

A

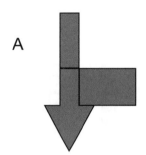

B

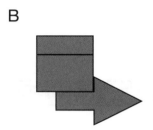

C

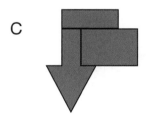

D

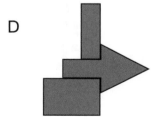

Answer [   ]

QUESTION 6

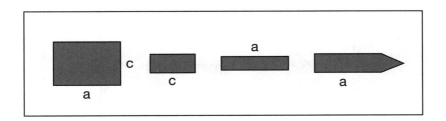

A    B

C   D

Answer [ ]

QUESTION 7

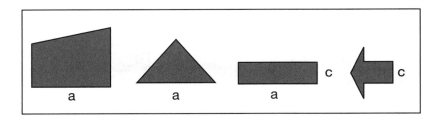

A 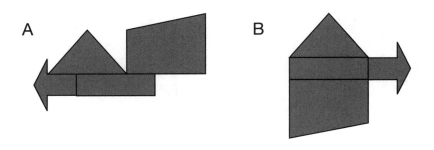 B

C 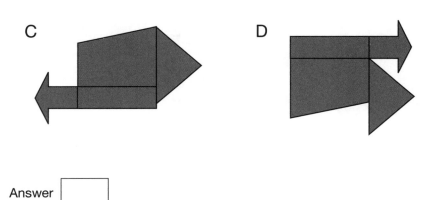 D

Answer [ ]

QUESTION 8

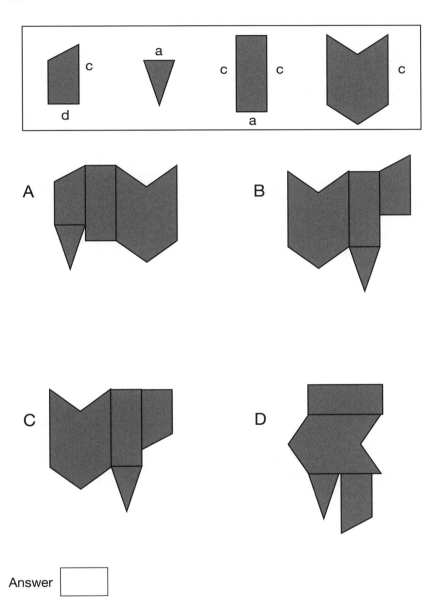

Answer [   ]

Now that you have completed the exercise take the time to work through
your answers carefully.

ANSWERS TO SPATIAL REASONING TEST EXERCISE 1

1. C
2. B
3. C
4. D
5. A
6. A
7. B
8. C

ROYAL AIR FORCE AIRMAN/AIRWOMAN TEST
SPATIAL REASONING TEST - EXERCISE 2

During the second spatial reasoning test that I've provided you with you will be required to look at 3-dimensional objects. You have to imagine the 3-dimensional objects rotated in a specific way and then match them up against a choice of examples.

Look at the 2 objects below:

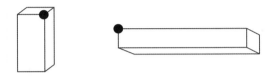

You now have to decide which of the 4 options provided demonstrates both objects rotated with the dot in the correct position. Look at the options below:

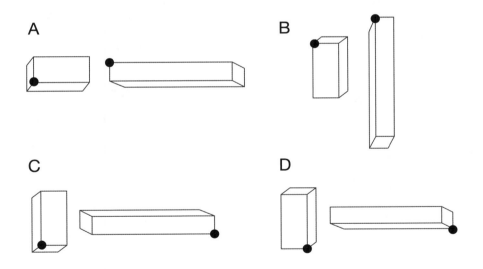

The correct answer is C

Now move on to spatial reasoning test exercise 2. You have 3 minutes in which to complete the 8 questions.

QUESTION 1

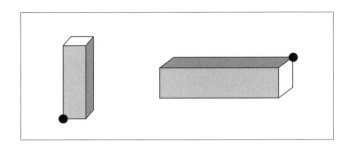

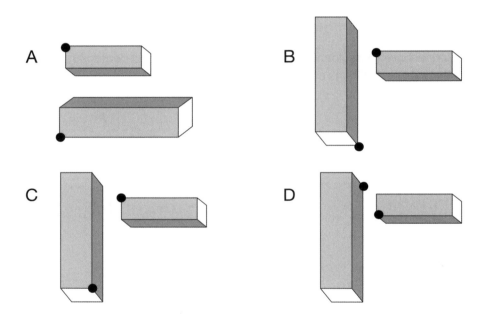

Answer

QUESTION 2

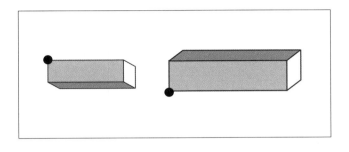

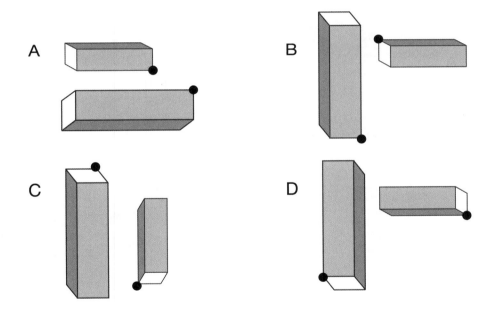

Answer

QUESTION 3

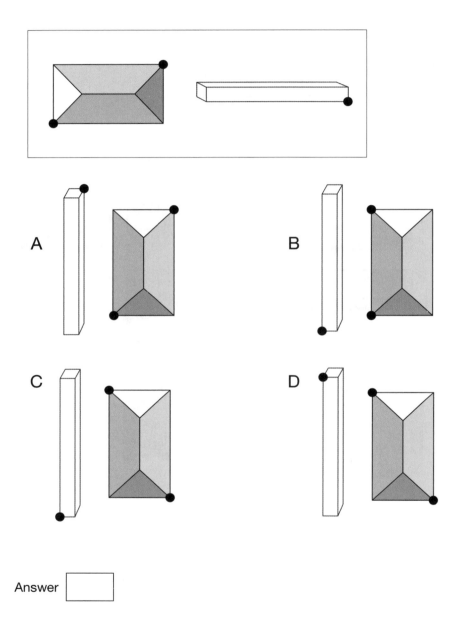

Answer [   ]

QUESTION 4

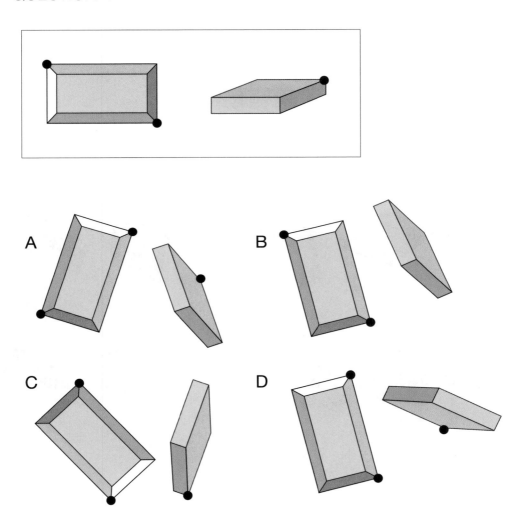

Answer [ ]

QUESTION 5

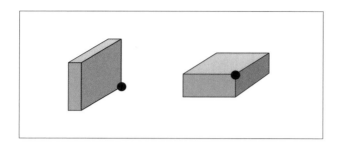

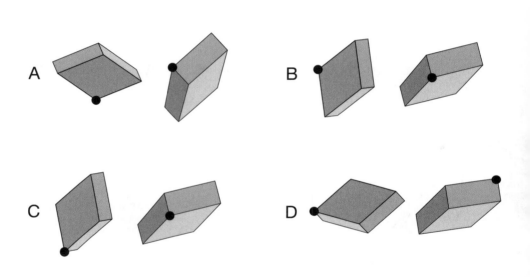

Answer ▢

QUESTION 6

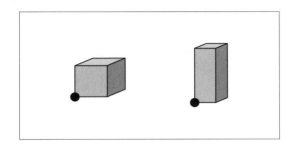

A 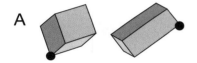   B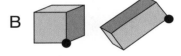

C 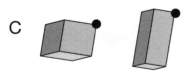   D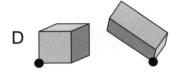

Answer [   ]

QUESTION 7

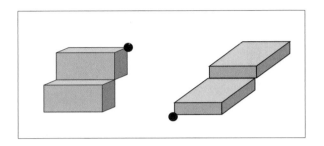

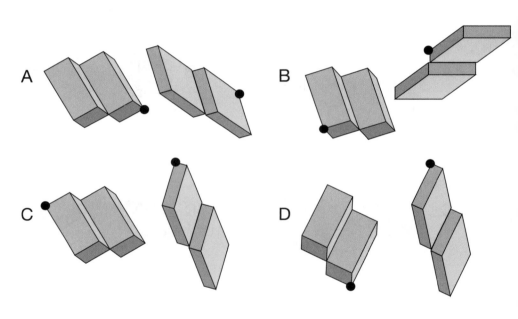

Answer [   ]

QUESTION 8

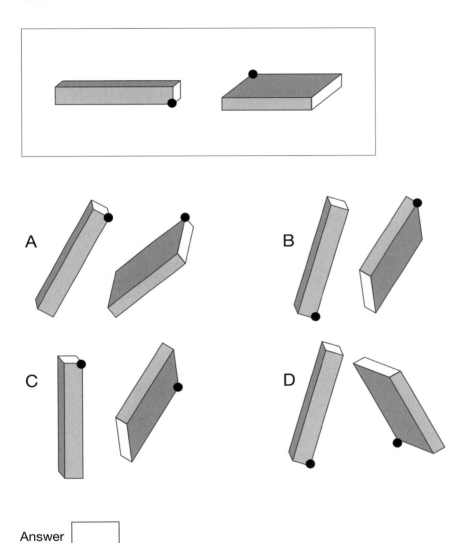

Answer

ANSWERS TO SPATIAL REASONING TEST EXERCISE 2

1. B
2. A
3. C
4. C
5. B
6. C
7. D
8. C

ROYAL AIR FORCE AIRMAN/AIRWOMAN TEST
ELECTRICAL COMPREHENSION TEST

During the AST you will be required to sit an Electrical Comprehension Test. The test itself is designed to assess your ability to work with different electrical concepts. On the following pages I have provided you with a number of sample questions to help you prepare for this test. Work through the questions as quickly as possible but remember to go back and check any questions that you may have got wrong. If you struggle to understand the concepts of electrical circuits and terminology then you may wish to purchase a booklet which will help you to understand how they work. You will be able to obtain a book from all good bookstores including www.amazon.co.uk.

In this particular exercise you have 10 minutes in which to answer the 20 questions.

ROYAL AIR FORCE AIRMAN/AIRWOMAN TEST
ELECTRICAL COMPREHENSION TEST - EXERCISE 1

QUESTION 1

In the following circuit, if switch A remains open, what will happen?

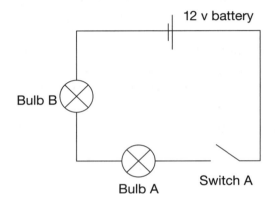

12 v battery

Bulb B

Bulb A

Switch A

A. Bulbs A and B will illuminate

B. Bulb A will illuminate only

C. No bulbs will illuminate

Answer

QUESTION 2

Which electrical component is the following a description of?

A safety device which will 'blow' (melt) if the current flowing through it exceeds a specified value.

A. Electron

B. Battery

C. Earth

D. Resistor

E. Fuse

Answer [   ]

QUESTION 3

Identify the following electrical symbol:

A. Fuse

B. Switch

C. Capacitor

D. Voltmeter

E. Variable resistor

Answer [   ]

QUESTION 4

Identify the following electrical symbol:

A. Capacitor

B. Ohmmeter

C. Ammeter

D. Bulb

E. Earphone

Answer [   ]

QUESTION 5

In the following circuit, if switch A remains open, what will happen?

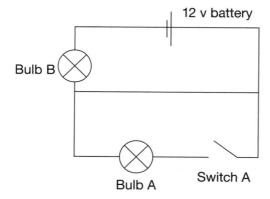

A. Bulb A and B will illuminate

B. Bulb A will illuminate only

C. Bulb B will illuminate only

D. No bulbs will illuminate

Answer [   ]

QUESTION 6

Which statement best describes the purpose of the following electrical symbol?

A. Used to measure current

B. Used to measure voltage

C. Used to measure resistance

D. Used to restrict the flow of current

Answer [   ]

QUESTION 7

Identify the following electrical symbol:

A. Neutron

B. Bulb

C. Inductor

D. Resistor

E. Capacitor

Answer [   ]

QUESTION 8

In the following circuit, if switch C remains open and switch A closes, what will happen?

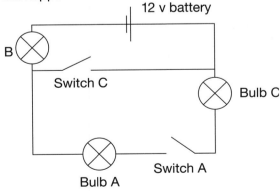

A. No bulbs will illuminate

B. Bulbs A and C will illuminate only

C. Bulbs A, B and C will illuminate

D. Bulb B will illuminate only

Answer

QUESTION 9

In the following circuit, if switch A remains open and switches B and C close, what will happen?

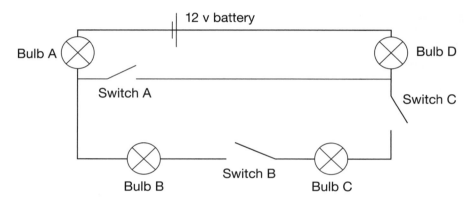

A. No bulbs will illuminate

B. Bulbs A and D will illuminate only

C. Bulbs B and C will illuminate only

D. Bulbs A, B and C will illuminate only

E. Bulbs A, B, C and D will illuminate

Answer

QUESTION 10

Identify the following electrical symbol:

A. AC supply

B. DC supply

C. Motor

D. Transformer

Answer

QUESTION 11

Identify the following electrical symbol:

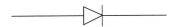

A. Ohm

B. Diode

C. Watt

D. Amplifier

Answer

QUESTION 12

In the following circuit, if switch A remains open and switches B closes, what will happen?

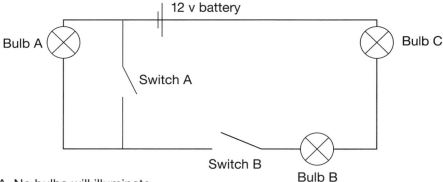

A. No bulbs will illuminate

B. Bulbs A, B and C will illuminate

C. Bulb A will illuminate only

D. Bulbs B and C will illuminate only

Answer

QUESTION 13

In the following circuit, if switch A closes and switch B remains open, what will happen?

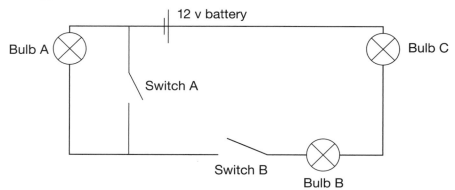

A. No bulbs will illuminate

B. Bulbs A, B and C will illuminate

C. Bulb A will illuminate only

D. Bulbs B and C will illuminate only

Answer

QUESTION 14

Identify the following electrical symbol:

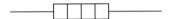

A. Transducer

B. Bell

C. Heater

D. LED

Answer

QUESTION 15

What will be the voltage at point X if the battery is 12 volts?

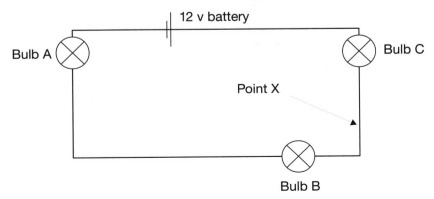

A. 0 Volts

B. 4 Volts

C. 6 Volts

D. 12 Volts

Answer

QUESTION 16

In the following electrical circuit, if switch B closes and switches A and C remain open, what will happen?

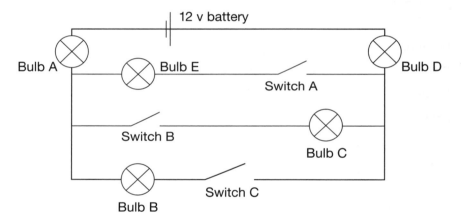

A. Bulbs A, B, C, D and E will illuminate.

B. Bulbs A, C, D and E will illuminate only.

C. Bulbs A, C and D will illuminate only.

D. No bulbs will illuminate.

Answer

QUESTION 17

In the following electrical circuit, if switches A and C close, what will happen?

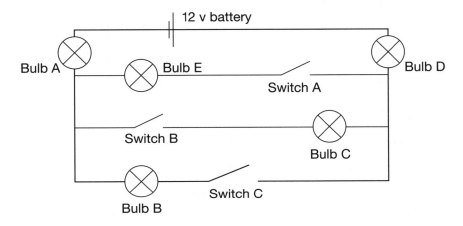

A. Bulbs A, B, D and E will illuminate.

B. Bulbs A, C, D and E will illuminate only.

C. Bulbs A, C and D will illuminate only.

D. No bulbs will illuminate.

Answer [   ]

QUESTION 18

In the following electrical circuit, if switch A closes, what will happen?

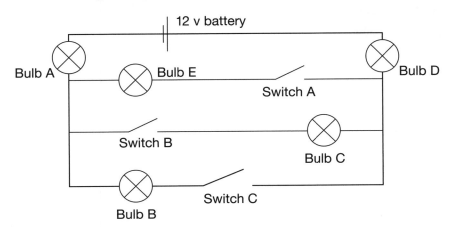

A. Bulbs A, D, and E will illuminate.

B. Bulb E will illuminate only.

C. Bulbs A, B, C, D and E will illuminate only.

D. No bulbs will illuminate.

Answer [   ]

QUESTION 19

If a fuse blows again after it has been replaced, what is the most likely cause?

A. The resistance in the circuit is too high.

B. The ground point has become disconnected.

C. Open circuit in component.

D. The current through the circuit is too high.

E. All of the above.

Answer [   ]

QUESTION 20

A possible cause of an open circuit would be?

A. A loose component mount.

B. A pin pushed out of a connector.

C. A corroded connection.

D. All of the above.

Answer [   ]

ANSWERS TO ELECTRICAL COMPREHENSION EXERCISE

1. C
2. E
3. E
4. B
5. C
6. A
7. C
8. C
9. E
10. D
11. B
12. B
13. A
14. C
15. D
16. C
17. A
18. A
19. D
20. D

ROYAL AIR FORCE AIRMAN/AIRWOMAN TEST
MEMORY TEST

During the Airman/Airwoman selection test you will be required to undertake a memory test. The test is usually in two parts. During the first part of the test you will be required to view a sequence of letters. The letters will appear on a screen for a period of time. After a period of time the sequence will disappear and you will then be required to answer questions relating to that sequence.

Let's assume that the sequence of letters looks like the following. Please note that during the real test the letters may appear individually over a set period of time and not collectively as per indicated below.

W	E	Q	X	R	E

Study the above sequence of letters for one minute only. Once the minute is up, cover the above sequence with your hand or a sheet of paper, and answer the following questions:

QUESTION 1

How many letter E's were there in the sequence?

Answer [ ]

QUESTION 2

How many letters were there in between the letter W and the letter X?

Answer [ ]

QUESTION 3

What letter was between the letter Q and the letter R?

Answer [ ]

Hopefully you managed to get the questions correct. Your ability to successfully pass this test will be dependant on how good your memory is.

ANSWERS TO SAMPLE TEST QUESTIONS

Question 1 – Two

Question 2 – Two

Question 3 – Letter X

In order to improve your ability during this test try the following sample exercise.

ROYAL AIR FORCE AIRMAN/AIRWOMAN TEST
MEMORY TEST – EXERCISE 1

F	A	Q	P	F	U

Study the above sequence of letters for one minute only. Once the minute is up, cover the above sequence with your hand or a sheet of paper, and answer the following questions:

QUESTION 1

How many letter F's were in the sequence?

Answer [   ]

QUESTION 2

How many letters were there in between the letter A and the letter U?

Answer [   ]

QUESTION 3

What was the first letter in the sequence?

Answer [   ]

ROYAL AIR FORCE AIRMAN/AIRWOMAN TEST
MEMORY TEST – EXERCISE 2

F	J	D	M	M	O

Study the above sequence of letters for one minute only. Once the minute is up, cover the above sequence with your hand or a sheet of paper, and answer the following questions:

QUESTION 1

How many letters were there in the entire sequence?

Answer

QUESTION 2

How many letters were there in between the letter F and the letter O?

Answer

QUESTION 3

What was the third letter in the sequence?

Answer

ROYAL AIR FORCE AIRMAN/AIRWOMAN TEST
MEMORY TEST – EXERCISE 3

G	B	S	K	E	G	Z

Study the above sequence of letters for one minute only. Once the minute is up, cover the above sequence with your hand or a sheet of paper, and answer the following questions:

QUESTION 1

How many letters were there in the entire sequence?

Answer [ ]

QUESTION 2

How many letter G's were there in the sequence?

Answer [ ]

QUESTION 3

How many letters were there in between the letter B and the letter Z?

Answer [ ]

ROYAL AIR FORCE AIRMAN/AIRWOMAN TEST
MEMORY TEST – EXERCISE 4

V	a	a	q	a	W	a

Study the above sequence of letters for one minute only. Once the minute is up, cover the above sequence with your hand or a sheet of paper, and answer the following questions:

QUESTION 1

How many capital letters were there in the sequence?

Answer

QUESTION 2

How many lower case (non capital) letters were there in the sequence?

Answer

QUESTION 3

How many letter a's were there between the letter V and W?

Answer

ROYAL AIR FORCE AIRMAN/AIRWOMAN TEST
MEMORY TEST – EXERCISE 5

N	r	s	T	z	X	Q	q

Study the above sequence of letters for one minute only. Once the minute is up, cover the above sequence with your hand or a sheet of paper, and answer the following questions:

QUESTION 1

How many capital letters were there in the sequence?

Answer

QUESTION 2

How many letters were there in the entire sequence?

Answer

QUESTION 3

How many vowels were there in the entire sequence?

Answer

ANSWERS TO MEMORY TEST EXERCISES

Memory test exercise 1

1. 2

2. 3

3. F

Memory test exercise 2

1. 6

2. 4

3. D

Memory test exercise 3

1. 7

2. 2

3. 4

Memory test exercise 4

1. 2

2. 5

3. 3

Memory test exercise 5

1. 4

2. 8

3. 0

ROYAL AIR FORCE AIRMAN/AIRWOMAN TEST
MEMORY TEST PART 2

During the second part of the test you will be required to view a number of different grids which contain coloured squares. Each grid will appear individually. Once the sequence of grids has disappeared you will be required to state which pattern the collective coloured squares make up from a number of different options.

Take a look at the following four grids. Please note: during the real test each grid will only appear one at a time and for a brief period. You will need to memorise the position of the coloured squares in each grid in order to answer the question.

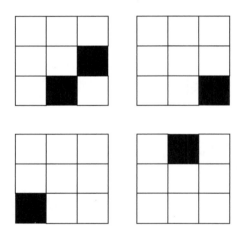

Once you have studied the grids cover them with your hand or a sheet of paper. Now decide from the following four options which grid contains the collective group of coloured squares from the four grids.

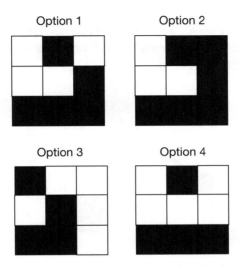

As you will see, **Option 1** accurately reflects the combined locations of the coloured squares from the initial four grids.

Once you understand what is required, move on to the following exercises.

ROYAL AIR FORCE AIRMAN/AIRWOMAN TEST
MEMORY TEST PART 2 – EXERCISE 1

QUESTION 1

Study the following grids for 10 seconds only. Then turn the page and decide from the four options available which grid contains the collective group of coloured squares from the grids.

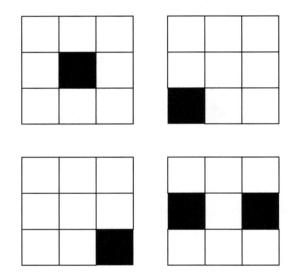

QUESTION 1 OPTIONS

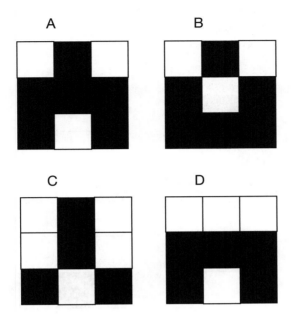

Answer

QUESTION 2

Study the following grids for 10 seconds only. Then turn the page and decide from the four options available which grid contains the collective group of coloured squares from the grids.

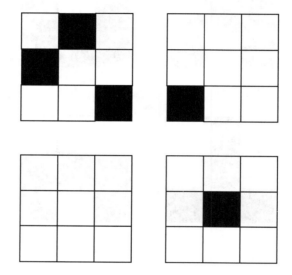

QUESTION 2 OPTIONS

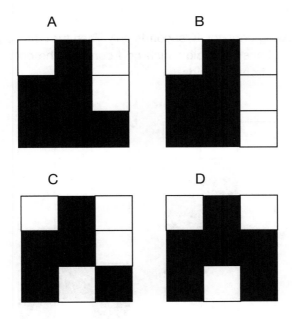

Answer

QUESTION 3

Study the following grids for 10 seconds only. Then turn the page and decide from the four options available which grid contains the collective group of coloured squares from the grids.

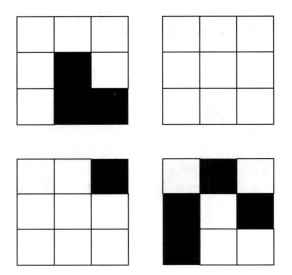

QUESTION 3 OPTIONS

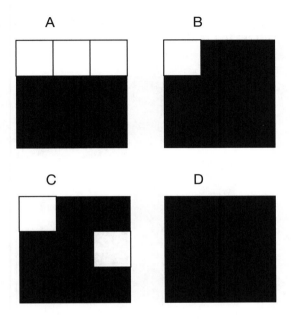

Answer

QUESTION 4

Study the following grids for 10 seconds only. Then turn the page and decide from the four options available which grid contains the collective group of coloured squares from the grids.

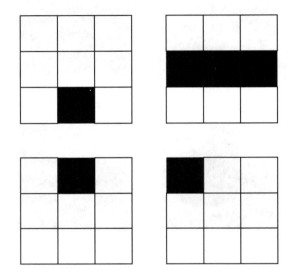

QUESTION 4 OPTIONS

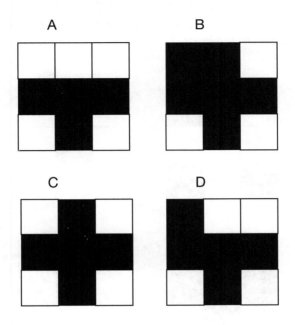

Answer [   ]

QUESTION 5

Study the following grids for 10 seconds only. Then turn the page and decide from the four options available which grid contains the collective group of coloured squares from the grids.

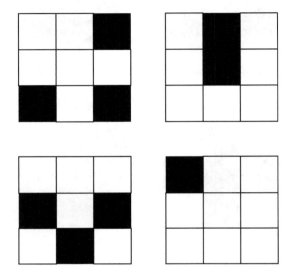

QUESTION 5 OPTIONS

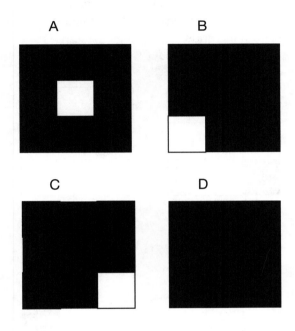

Answer

QUESTION 6

Study the following grids for 10 seconds only. Then turn the page and decide from the four options available which grid contains the collective group of coloured squares from the grids.

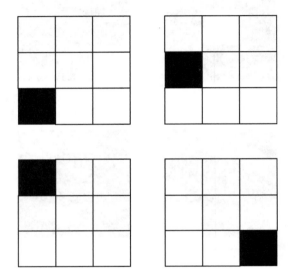

QUESTION 6 OPTIONS

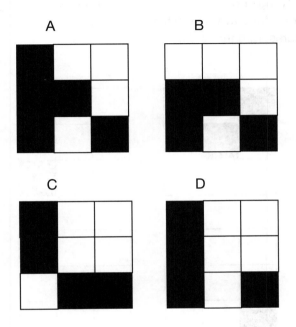

Answer [   ]

QUESTION 7

Study the following grids for 10 seconds only. Then turn the page and decide from the four options available which grid contains the collective group of coloured squares from the grids.

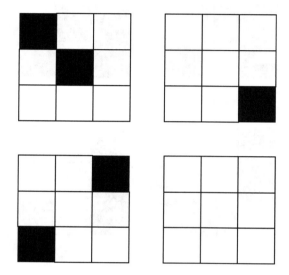

QUESTION 7 OPTIONS

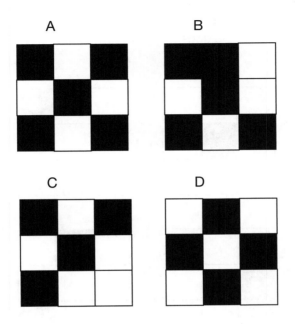

Answer [   ]

QUESTION 8

Study the following grids for 10 seconds only. Then turn the page and decide from the four options available which grid contains the collective group of coloured squares from the grids.

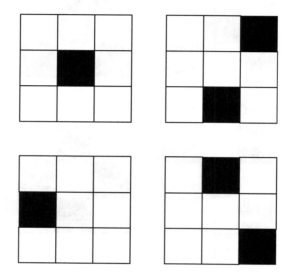

QUESTION 8 OPTIONS

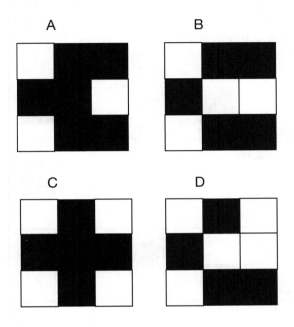

Answer

QUESTION 9

Study the following grids for 10 seconds only. Then turn the page and decide from the four options available which grid contains the collective group of coloured squares from the grids.

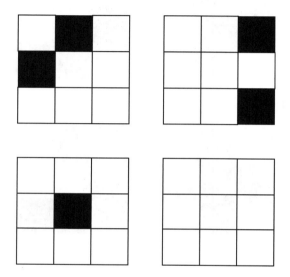

QUESTION 9 OPTIONS

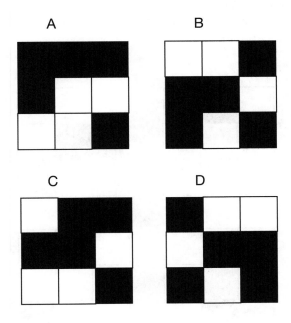

A   B

C   D

Answer

QUESTION 10

Study the following grids for 10 seconds only. Then turn the page and decide from the four options available which grid contains the collective group of coloured squares from the grids.

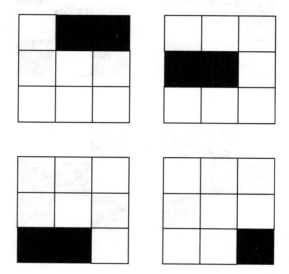

QUESTION 10 OPTIONS

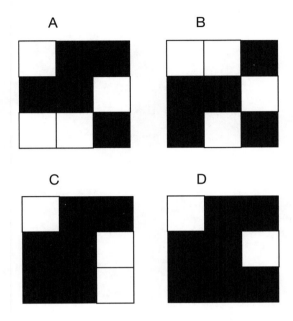

Answer ☐

ANSWERS TO MEMORY TEST PART 2

1. D
2. C
3. B
4. B
5. D
6. D
7. A
8. A
9. C
10. D

OVERCOMING TEST NERVES

The majority of people who are required to undertake any form of test will get nervous. This is only natural and without some degree of nerves you won't be able to perform to the best of your ability. However, some people will unfortunately experience uncontrollable nerves. It is only natural to feel nervous before a test but there are a number of things that you can do to get over these nerves. To begin with, lets take a look at a few of the more common pre-test anxieties:

• Feeling generally nervous and anxious

• Sweaty hands and palms

• Trembling voice

• Sore head

• Aching muscles

• Dry mouth

• Increased heart beat

• Shaky hands

I can remember taking my driving test at the age of 17 and feeling a few of the above symptoms. In the build up to the test I had worried myself so much that eventually I thought, "What's the point in all of this? It's only a driving test, who cares if I fail?" I had seriously reached the point where I didn't really care anymore whether I passed or failed. Now this is probably going to sound stupid, but this change in attitude actually worked in my favour. I performed a lot better during the driving test, simply because inside I had stopped caring, and therefore the nerves went out of the window. Now I am not saying that you shouldn't care about your tests, because that would be silly. But what I am saying is that you can only do so much practice and you can only do so many mock tests. Once you have done sufficient preparation for the tests, and you will know when that time has come, then it is pointless worrying anymore about it. Do your study, do your preparation, and then go to the test centre feeling free, calm and relaxed, and trust me, you will perform a whole lot better!

Visualising the test before you attend it

This is a great method that works for many people. Before you attend the test, try and visualise the entire process. Sit down in your favourite armchair and close your eyes. Think about driving to the test centre with plenty of time to spare. You arrive early at the venue and sit in the car park composing yourself and reading through a number of sample test questions. When you walk into the test centre you are standing tall, smiling and feeling relaxed and confident. You introduce yourself in a polite manner and shake the hands of the assessor. You sit down in the chair and listen carefully to all instructions. Once the test commences you work quickly, yet calmly, and you try your hardest to answer all of the questions accurately. Once you have completed the test you take the time to go back through your answers.

The above method is a fantastic way of focusing yourself prior to any test. If you try to visualise the entire process being successful before the event starts, then this will put you in the correct frame of mind.

Alternative testing resources

I hope that you have found this guide to be a great use in your preparation for the Armed Forces tests. You can also obtain further testing resources from the website www.how2become.co.uk including sample online testing questions.

THE **TESTING** SERIES
expert advice on test preparation

Visit www.how2become.co.uk to find more titles and courses that will help you to pass any job interview or selection process:

• Online Armed forces testing

• Job interview DVDs and books

• 1-day intensive career training courses

• Psychometric testing books and CDs.

WWW.HOW2BECOME.CO.UK